The (

CW00822201

Cy

2001/2002

Use this guide with the official route map
available from Sustrans 0117 929 0888

Gina Farncombe

Curlew Press

| 8th Edition | *C2C & Reivers* |
| | *Accommodation Guide Book* |

Edited by   Gina Farncombe

Published by   Curlew Press
                 Crookwath Cottage
                 Dockray, Penrith,
                 Cumbria CA11 0LG
                 017684 82633

e-mail   gfarncombe@aol.com
Web page   cumbria.com/accom/cycling.htm

                 © Curlew Press 2001
                 ISBN 1-901224-06-6

Distributed by   Cordee Books and Maps
                 3a de Montfort Street
                 Leicester LE1 7HD
                 Tel 0116 254 3579

Front cover   Sustrans
Back cover   Philip Nixon

INTRODUCTION

Welcome to the C2C B&B Guide. This guide is designed to be used with the C2C Sustrans Map obtainable from Sustrans, 35 King Street, Bristol BS1 4DZ, tel. 0117 929 0888.

Your hosts have all been chosen for their understanding of the cyclist's needs, a warm welcome, acceptance of muddy legs, a secure place for your bike and provision of a meal either with them or at a nearby pub. Have a great holiday!

The route is designed to be tackled west to east to take advantage of the prevailing winds. Both the Sustrans map and this accommodation guide run from west to east.

Please try to book accommodation, meals and packed lunches in advance, and do not arrive unannounced expecting beds and meals to be available! If you have to cancel a booking, please give the proprietor as much notice as you can so that the accommodation can be re-let. Your deposit may be forfeited: this is at the discretion of the proprietor.

Suggestions for additional addresses are most welcome, together with your comments.

Please note: the information given in the Guide was correct at the time of printing and was as supplied by the proprietors. No responsibility can be accepted by the Independent B&B Guide as to completeness or accuracy, nor for any loss arising as a result. It is advisable to check the relevant details when booking.

Where do I start the C2C ....?

The best way to cycle the C2C is from West to East coast. If you want to return to the West Coast via the Reivers Route the gradients will be to your advantage.

By Train
To get to Whitehaven or Workington by train you must change on to a local line at CARLISLE. The journey takes about 1 hour. It follows the coastline and is dramatic and spectacular. Remember, it is essential to book your bike on the train well in advance.

Train enquiries	0345 484 950
Cycle reservations	
& bookings	08457 222 333

Return by Train
From Sunderland, continue to cycle up the coast to the main-line station at Newcastle. Remember, the local train from Sunderland will only take a total of 2 bikes. You will need to make special arrangements for more bikes.

By Car
If you have to come by car most landladies will allow you to leave your vehicle with them. There is secure long-term car parking in Whitehaven; 'phone the TIC on 01946 852939, or use one of the taxi services on page 123 or cycle back on the Reivers Route!

Note: Back-up vehicles are strongly advised to use main roads in order to keep the C2C as traffic free as possible.

CONTENTS

Accommodation
place names (west-east)

C - 2 - C CYCLE ROUTE - WESTERN HALF

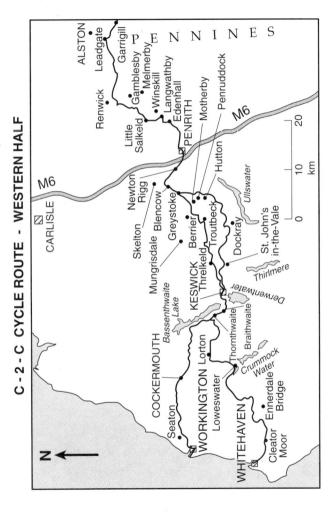

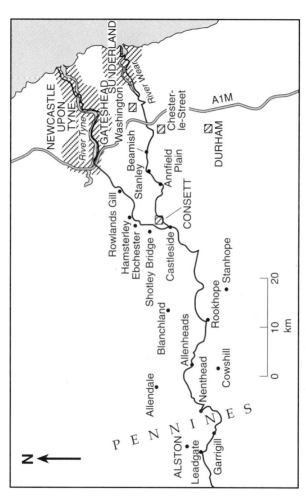

C - 2 - C CYCLE ROUTE - EASTERN HALF

N

NEWCASTLE UPON TYNE
River Tyne
GATESHEAD
SUNDERLAND
River Wear
Washington
A1M
Chester-le-Street
DURHAM
Beamish
Stanley
Anfield Plain
CONSETT
Rowlands Gill
Hamsterley
Ebchester
Shotley Bridge
Castleside
Rookhope
Stanhope
Blanchland
Allenheads
Rookhope
Allendale
Nenthead
Cowshill
ALSTON
Leadgate
Garrigill

PENNINES

0   10   20
      km

7

TOPOGRAPHICAL CROSS-SECTIONS OF THE C-2-C CYCLE ROUTE

The C-2-C is 140 miles in length. It is strongly advised to ride the route from West to East, giving the benefit of the prevailing westerly winds at your back. As seen from the topographical sections, the uphill biking is short and sharp, and the downhill biking is long and gentle.

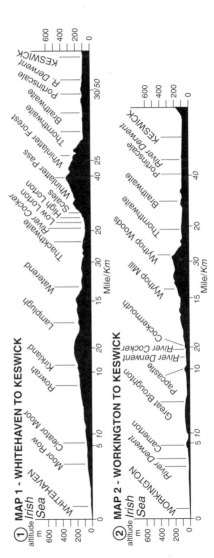

① MAP 1 - WHITEHAVEN TO KESWICK

② MAP 2 - WORKINGTON TO KESWICK

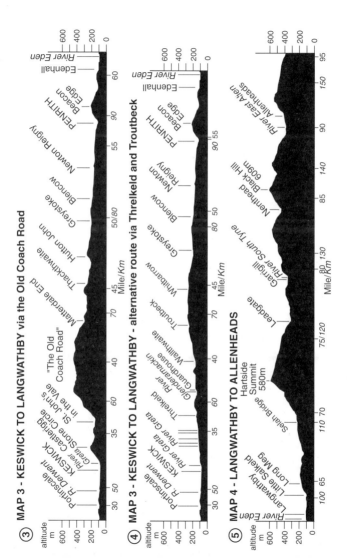

③ MAP 3 - KESWICK TO LANGWATHBY via the Old Coach Road

altitude m: 600 400 200 0

River Eden — Edenhall — PENRITH — Beacon Edge — Newton Reigny — Blencow — Greystoke — Hutton John — Thackthwaite — Matterdale End — "The Old Coach Road" — St. John's in the Vale — Castlerigg Stone Circle — KESWICK — R. Derwent — Portinscale

Mile/Km: 60 · 90 · 55 · 50/80 · 45 · 70 · 40 · 60 · 35 · 50 · 30

④ MAP 3 - KESWICK TO LANGWATHBY - alternative route via Threlkeld and Troutbeck

altitude m: 600 400 200 0

River Eden — Edenhall — PENRITH — Beacon Edge — Newton Reigny — Blencow — Greystoke — Whitbarrow — Troutbeck — Wallthwaite — Guardhouse — Glenderamackin — River Greta — Threlkeld — River Greta — KESWICK — R. Derwent — Portinscale

Mile/Km: 90 · 55 · 80 · 50 · 45 · 70 · 40 · 60 · 35 · 50 · 30

⑤ MAP 4 - LANGWATHBY TO ALLENHEADS

altitude m: 600 400 200 0

River East Allen — Allenheads — Nenthead — Black Hill 609m — Garrigill — River South Tyne — Leadgate — Selah Bridge — Hartside Summit 580m — Langwathby — Little Salkeld — Long Meg — River Eden

Mile/Km: 95 · 150 · 90 · 140 · 85 · 130 · 80 · 75/120 · 70 · 110 · 65 · 100 · 60

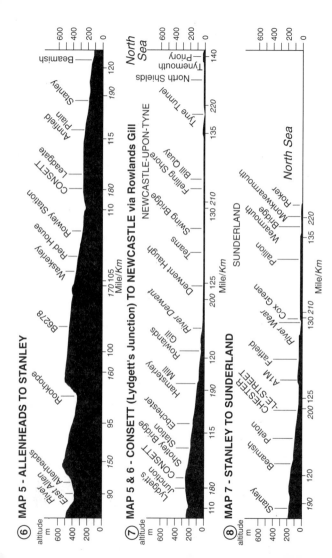

6 MAP 5 - ALLENHEADS TO STANLEY

altitude m: 600, 400, 200, 0

Beamish
Stanley
Annfield Plain
Leadgate
CONSETT
Rowley Station
Red House
Waskerley
B6278
Rookhope
East Allen
River Allen
Allenheads

Mile/Km: 120, 190, 115, 180, 110 105, 170, 100, 160, 95, 150, 90

7 MAP 5 & 6 - CONSETT (Lydgett's Junction) TO NEWCASTLE via Rowlands Gill

altitude m: 600, 400, 200, 0

North Sea
Tynemouth Priory
North Shields
Tyne Tunnel
NEWCASTLE-UPON-TYNE
Felling Shore
Bill Quay
Swing Bridge
Teams
Derwent Haugh
River Derwent
Rowlands Gill
Hamsterley Mill
Ebchester
Shotley Bridge Station
CONSETT
Lydgett's Junction

Mile/Km: 140, 220, 135, 130 210, 200 125, 120, 190, 115, 180, 110

8 MAP 7 - STANLEY TO SUNDERLAND

altitude m: 600, 400, 200, 0

North Sea
Roker
Monkwearmouth Bridge
Wearmouth
SUNDERLAND
Pallion
Cox Green
River Wear
Fatfield
A1M
CHESTER-LE-STREET
Pelton
Beamish
Stanley

Mile/Km: 220, 135, 130 210, 200 125, 120, 190

WHITEHAVEN

Whitehaven bay

The town reached its peak of prosperity in the 1740s and 50s with outward trade of coal to Dublin and imports of tobacco from America and rum and sugar from the West Indies. There were early connections with the slave trade together with people settling in America. It was the third busiest port after London and Bristol. The Lowther family laid out the grid pattern for the

Georgian town in the late 1690s. Whitehaven`s most notable scientist was William Brownrigg who studied the explosive mine-gas "fire damp". George Washington's grandmother, Mildred WarnerGale, lived in Whitehaven. Don't forget to dip your bike wheel in the Irish Sea! There is a convenient slipway on the harbour front.

The Beacon Visitor Centre

Whitehaven Tourist Information

PLACES OF INTEREST

Michael Moon's, Roper Street	Bookshop & Gallery: one of the largest bookshops in Cumbria, "vast and gloriously eccentric!"
The Beacon	Local maritime and industrial history within the Harbour Gallery

EATING OUT

Casa Romana	132 Queen Street. Good food & fun. 01946 591901
St Nicholas Centre	St Nicholas Gardens, Lowther Street 01946 64404
The New Expresso	22 Market Place: will do sandwiches to order. Please phone 01946 591548

CYCLE SHOPS

Kershaw's Cycles	125 Queen Street 01946 590700
Mark Taylor Cycles	5/6 New Street 01946 692252

*C2C Route Features: as you leave Whitehaven you will join the Whitehaven-Rowrah cycle path which links the sea to the fells. The railway line was built in the 1850s to carry limestone, coal and iron; it is now a sculpture trail interpreting the geology and industrial history of the region. Further down the C2C the route takes you past the **Whinlatter Visitor Centre**, between Lorton and Braithwaite. Here you are in the midst of England's only mountain forest. It contains a wealth of forest habitat information and is well worth a visit if time and energy allow. They have a good tea room too.*

Whitehaven

Mrs Armstrong

Glen Ard Guest House, Inkerman Terrace, Whitehaven, CA28 7TY

Telephone	**01946 692249**
Rooms	1 single + 2 double + 2 twin + 2 family
B&B	£15.00
Packed lunch	£3.50
Distance from C2C	¼ mile Pub nearby

"Family-run guest-house with a private car park only ¼ mile from the C2C route. Early breakfast available if requested."

Mrs C. M. Oliver

Glenlea House, Glenlea Hill, Lowca, Whitehaven, Cumbria CA28 6PS

Telephone	**01946 693873** Fax 01946 694350
Rooms	3 single + 4 double + 4 twin + 3 family
B&B	£17.50 - £25.00
Evening meal	£8.50-£10.50 Packed lunch £3.50
Distance from C2C	On route Pub 1 mile

"Family-run licensed guest-house. Private car park. Early breakfast available for those wishing to make the most of the day. We are happy to pick up cyclists from the station."

(See advertisement on page 79)

Waverley Hotel

Tangier Street, Whitehaven, Cumbria CA28 7UX.

Telephone	**01946 694375** Fax 01946 691577
Email	waverleyhotel@tinyworld.co.uk
Rooms	10 single + 10 double
B&B	From £20.00 - £37.00
Evening meal	Available Packed lunch available
Distance from C2C	¼ mile Licensed restaurant

"300-year-old hotel in centre of historic Whitehaven. All rooms have colour TV and tea/coffee-making facilities. Very near to bus and train station."

Whitehaven

T. Todd   The Mansion, Old Woodhouse,
                       Whitehaven, Cumbria CA28 9LN

Telephone   **01946 61860**   Fax 01946 691270
Rooms   10 double rooms *(8 en-suite)*
B&B   From £11.00 - £15.00
Evening meal   £4.00-£6.00   Packed Lunch £3.00
Distance from C2C   600m   Pub nearby

"Friendly B&B. Five minutes from the town centre. Hot tub and sauna and sun deck. William Wordsworth stayed here!"

Frizington

Mrs E.A. Hall   14 Lingley Fields, Frizington, Near
                       Whitehaven, Cumbria CA26 3RU

Telephone   **01946 811779**
Rooms   1 twins + 1 family
B&B   £16.00-£20.00
Evening meal   £8.00 *(please book ahead)*
Packed lunch   £2.50   Distance from C2C 1 mile

"Village house set in cottage-style garden. Comfortable, non-smoking accommodation. Choice of breakfasts. Drying facilities and secure undercover cycle parking available."

Egremont

A. Ciereszko   Bookwell Garth Guest House, 16
                       Bookwell, Egremont, CA22 2LS.

Telephone/fax   **01946 820271**   Mob **07879 660096**
Rooms   5 single, 7 twin + 1 family
B&B   From £12.00 - £16.00
Evening meal   On request Packed Lunch £3.00
Distance from C2C   1½ miles from start   Pub nearby

"Recently renovated Georgian residence. Sauna, jacuzzi and sunbed available. Friendly and informal. Courtesy pick-up if needed, off-street parking."

WORKINGTON

Helena Thompson Museum

Some parts of the town date back to Roman times. Local iron and steel-making helped Workington to expand into a major industrial 18th-century town and port. Famous names linked to the town are Henry Bessemer who introduced his revolutionary steel-making process and Mary Queen of Scots who sheltered in Workington Hall in 1568 on her flight from Scotland. The Hall is now ruined, but is open in summer and is a short distance from the Helena Thompson Museum.

PLACES OF INTEREST

Helena Thompson Museum Park End Road: a local history gallery together with the famous Clifton dish.

Workington Hall Apparently haunted by Henry Curwen!

EATING OUT

Impressions 173 Vulcans Lane: Good traditional English food 01900 605446

Super Fish 20 Pow St 01900 604916

CYCLE SHOPS

Traffic Lights Bikes 35 Washington St 01900 603283

New Bike Shop 18-20 Market Place 01900 603337

Workington

Mrs Caroline Nelson

Morven House Hotel, Siddick Road, Workington, Cumbria CA14 1LE

Telephone/Fax	**01900 602118**
Rooms	4 twin + 2 double + 2 single + 1 family
B&B	£19.50-£24.00
Evening meal	£10.00 Packed lunch £4.00
Distance from C2C	On route Pub nearby

ETB 3 diamonds *"A relaxed, informal atmosphere, an ideal stopover for C2C participants near start. Car park and secure cycle storage."* **(See advertisement on page 78.)**

Mrs Hazel Hardy

Silverdale, 17 Banklands, Workington, Cumbria CA14 3EL

Telephone	**01900 61887**
Rooms	2 twins + 2 single
B&B	£13.50-£15.00
Distance from C2C	On route Pub nearby

(No smoking in bedrooms please.) *"Large Victorian house, quiet location, wash-basins in all bedrooms, bathroom has shower, comfy TV lounge, centrally placed, good parking."*

Ennerdale Bridge

Mr Norman Stanfield	The Shepherds Arms Hotel, Ennerdale Bridge, Cleator, Cumbria CA23 3AR
Telephone/Fax	**01946 861249**
Email	enquiries@shepherdsarmshotel.co.uk
Rooms	1 family + 3 double + 3 twin + 1 single
B&B	£28.00-£30.50
Evening meal	£4.00-£14.50 Packed Lunch £4.00
Distance from C2C	1¼ miles Hotel has Public Bar

2 Star Hotel. *"The ideal place to relax, public bar, good beer guide, extensive bar menu, large vegetarian selection, comfortable bedrooms, open fires. Safe cycle storage."*

Lorton

Mrs C. Edmunds	Meadow Bank, High Lorton, Cockermouth, Cumbria CA13 9UG
Telephone/Fax	**01900 85315**
Rooms	1 double + 1 twin en-suite
B&B	£18.00-£19.00
Packed lunch	£3.50
Distance from C2C	200 yds Pub 0.5 mile

(No smoking please.) *"Comfortable detached house in picturesque village of Lorton, 4 miles from Cockermouth, 10 from Keswick. Excellent, of a very high standard, most welcoming."*

Mrs Armstrong	Terrace Farm, Lorton, Cockermouth, cumbria CA13 9TX
Telephone	**01900 85278**
Rooms	1 twin/single + 2 family *(all en-suite)*
B&B	£19.00-£22.50
Distance from C2C	c. ½ mile Pub nearby

2 Diamonds Commended. *"Homely welcome at our family-run hill-farm set in secluded village location with superb Lakeland fell views. Good pub food within walking distance."*

COCKERMOUTH

Cockermouth Castle

One of only two "Gem Towns" in the Lake District, Cockermouth is full of fine Georgian architecture and is set on the confluence of two famous salmon rivers: the Derwent and the Cocker. The historic town of Cockermouth has long held an attraction for writers, poets and artists. It is the birthplace of William and Dorothy Wordsworth and has a bustling community air about it. The smell of brewing hops often pervades the air and makes a visit to the pub tempting! The town has had its fair share of troubled times from the Border Raiders and it played host to the fugitive Mary Queen of Scots.

Wordsworth House

Cockermouth

PLACES OF INTEREST

Castlegate House	Frequent exhibitions of interesting contemporary artists 01900 822149
Printing House Museum	'Hands on' experience!

EATING OUT

The Quince & Medlar	13 Castle St: award-winning vegetarian food 01900 823579
Cheers	Main St: Wholesome home-made pasta and pizzas 01900 822109

CYCLE SHOPS

The Wordsworth Hotel Bike Hire	Main St 01900 822757
Derwent Cycles	4 Market Place 01900 822113

C2C Route Features: take care of the very steep descent through Wythop Woods down to Bassenthwaite lakeside. Thornthwaite Gallery is well worth a visit.

Cockermouth

John and **Susan Graham**	Rose Cottage, Lorton Road, Cockermouth, Cumbria CA13 9DX
Telephone/Fax	**01900 822189**
Rooms	3 double + 3 twin + 2 family + 1 single *(all en-suite)*
B&B	£23.00-£30.00
3-course Dinner	£15.00 Packed lunch £5.00
Distance from C2C	¼ mile Pubs nearby

(No smoking in bedrooms please.)
3 Diamonds ETB
"Converted 18th-c Inn, family-run, garden, private car park, secure bicycle storage, warm and friendly atmosphere."

Vincent **Fernandez**	Castlegate Guest House, 6 Castlegate Cumbria CA13 9EU
Telephone/Fax	**01900 826749 mob. 0771 382 5144**
E-mail	**vince@vjfernandez.fsnet.co.uk**
Rooms	3 double + 1 twin + 2 triples
B&B	£17.50-£20.00
Packed lunch	£3.50 *(prior notice please)*
Distance from C2C	On route Pubs nearby

"A listed georgian house. Central position and on cycle routes. Popular with cyclists, walkers and tourists for 17 years. Secure store for bikes."

Newlands Valley

Tish & Tex **Gowing**	The Swinside Inn, Newlands Valley, Keswick, Cumbria CA12 5UE.
Telephone/Fax	**01768778253**
Rooms	1 single, 2 doubles, 2 twins + 1 family
B&B	£20.00-£25.00
Evening meal	£5.00-£12.00 Packed lunch £3.50
Distance from C2C	0.5 miles

3 Diamonds. *"Superb location. Clean spacious bedrooms. Most en-suite. Excellent bar meals. Real logfires in winter. An old world country pub set in a beautiful Lakeland Valley."*

Swaledales

Braithwaite

Chris White	Applegarth, Braithwaite, Keswick, Cumbria CA12 5TD
Telephone	**01768778462**
Rooms	2 double + 1 single
B&B	£16.00 Packed lunch - £3.00
Distance from C2C	On route Pub nearby

"Small friendly B&B on C2C route. All cyclists' needs on hand. Very popular so book early!"

KESWICK

Derwentwater

Sandwiched between Derwentwater, Blencathra and Skiddaw, Keswick has a fantastic setting. It became prosperous in the 16th century due to the mining of copper, lead, silver and iron. Mining engineers were imported from Germany: they were treated with suspicion by the locals and forced to make their homes on Derwent Island, but they overcame the hostility as German surnames can still be found amongst the local population. Graphite discovered in Borrowdale in the 1500s gave birth to the famous Cumberland Pencil Company.

The Moot Hall (now the TIC)

Keswick Tourist Information

PLACES OF INTEREST

The Cumberland Pencil Museum West of town centre 017687 73626

Cars of the Stars Town centre: vintage cars of famous stars 017687 73757

EATING OUT

Lakeland Pedlar By central car park: combined tea/bike shop 017687 74492

Maysons Lake Rd: importers of Eastern goods and excellent food 017687 74104

CYCLE SHOPS

The Stores, Braithwaite Mr Hindmarch does cycle repairs in the village of Braithwaite 017687 78273

Keswick Mountain Bikes Behind Pencil Museum: they do hot-air ballooning too! 017687 75202

C2C Route Features: the route follows the old railway line which crosses and re-crosses the dramatic river Greta. The alternative Old Coach Road route passes **Castlerigg** *: Don't miss this atmospheric stone circle!*

Castlerigg Stone Circle

Keswick

S. Trense	"Rivendell", 23 Helvellyn Street, Keswick, Cumbria CA12 4EN
Telephone	**01768773822**
Rooms	2 double + 3 twin + 1 family + 1single
B&B	£17.00-£21.00
Evening meal	£10.00 Packed lunch £3.50
Distance from C2C	On route Pub nearby

(No smoking please.) "Newly re-furbished guesthouse. Lockable bike shed, drying facilities, with very high standard of comfort."

Gina & Graham Burn	Harvington House, 19 Church Street, Keswick, Cumbria CA12 4DX
Telephone	**017687 75582**
E-mail	**enquiries@harvingtonhouse.freeserve.co.uk**
Rooms	2 single + 2 double + 1 twin
B&B	From £17.00-21.00*(no smoking please)*
Distance from C2C	On route Pub 5 mins

Hotel & Caterers Association Inspection *"Do you need a C2C stopover, or a base for some excellent mountain biking? Friendly relaxed B&B, secure bike storage and hearty breakfasts. Then give us a call!"*

Mrs K Wells	Ivy Lodge, 32 Penrith Road, Keswick Cumbria CA12 4HA
Telephone	**017687 75747 Fax 017687 75642**
E-mail	**peter@ivy-lodgefreeserve.co.uk**
Rooms	2 double + 2 twin
B&B	£18.50-£23.00 Evening Meal £10.00
Distance from C2C	500 yds Town 3 mins

"Convenient for parks, theatre and lake. Superb en-suite bedrooms. Drying room & lock up for cycles."

Keswick

Mrs B.J. Harbage   Glaramara Guest House, 9 Acorn St,
Keswick, Cumbria CA12 4EA

Telephone/Fax	**017687 73216/75255**
Mobile	**0411 763 019**
Website:	**www.keswickcycleactiveguesthouse.co.uk**
e-mail	**keswick9glaramara@madasafish.com**
Rooms	1 single + 2 doubles + 1 twin + 1 family
B&B	From £18.00-£22 Packed Lunch £3.50

"Cosy, warm guest house with en-suite & drying facilities. Bike hire, storage, minor spares and repairs. Owners are mountain bikers and have local knowlege of good cyling."

Keith & Tracy Baker   Hall Garth, 37 Blencathra Street,
Keswick, Cumbria CA12 4HX

Telephone	**017687 72627**	
Rooms	1 single + 4 double + 2 twin + 1 family	
B&B	From £18.00-£20.00	
Evening meal	Available	Pubs nearby
Distance from C2C	On route	

4 Diamonds *"Homely guest house, centrally located for town, lake, fells, all rooms with T.V. tea/ coffee, hairdryers, hearty breakfast, children welcome, secure cycle storage."*

Keswick

Bill and Elizabeth Riding

	Derwentdale Guest House, 8 Blencathra Street, Keswick, Cumbria CA12 4HP
Telephone	**017687 74187**.
Rooms	3 double + 2 single + 1 twin
B&B	£17.50-£21.00 *(some en-suite)*
Packed lunch	£4.50
Distance from C2C	On route Pub nearby

(No smoking please.) **3 Diamonds** *"Friendly, comfortable, centrally-heated guest-house. Colour TV, tea/coffeemaking facilities, hair dryers, vegetarian cooking, close to town centre."*

Sonja Cooper

	Cranford House, 18 Eskin Street, Keswick, Cumbria CA12 4DG
Telephone	**017687 71017**
e-mail	sonja@cranfordhouse.co.uk
Rooms	2 single + 4 double + 4 twin
B&B	£17.00-£20 Packed lunch £3.50
Distance from C2C	On route Pub nearby

(No smoking please.) *"Friendly, relaxed B&B. No ornaments or doilies! King-size beds, en suite available. Lounge with open fire. 5 minutes walk from town centre. Secure bike storage and drying facilities."*

The Proprietor

	The Skiddaw Hotel, Main Street Keswick, Cumbria CA12 5BN.
Telephone	**017687 72071 Fax 017687 74850**
Rooms	16 double + 11 twin + 6 family + 7 single
B&B	£35.00-£41.00
Evening meal	From £12.95 Packed lunch £4.50
Distance from C2C	On route

3 AA Star + 4 Diamonds Highly commended. *"Keswick town centre. Very comfortable hotel with free in-house saunas.*

Threlkeld

Chris and Caroline Briggs

Scales Farm Country Guest House.
Scales, Threlkeld, Keswick, CA12 4SY

Telephone/Fax **01768 79660**
Rooms 3 double + 1 family ı 2 twin
B&B From £24.00   Packed lunch £4.50
Distance from C2C On route   Pub adjacent

ETB 2 Crown Highly Commended. "*A welcoming traditional fells farmhouse oozing charm and character.* "

Scales

The White Horse Excellent pub for food & drink, no B&B

Mungrisdale

Jim & Margaret Hodge

The Mill Inn, Mungrisdale, nr Penrith, Cumbria CA11 0XR

Telephone/Fax **01768 79632**
e-mail margaret@millinn2.fsnet.co.uk
Rooms 1 single + 4 double + 3 twin
B&B £25.00-£35.00
Meals £4.00-£20.00, served all day
Packed lunch £4.00   Public Bar
Distance from C2C On new amended route

(Smoking in bar only please.) **3 Diamonds AA QQQ.** "*Traditional 16th-c Inn. Beautiful location. Log fire, warm welcome, Excellent accommodation, home-made food, and cask ales. Lock-ups available.* "

The Mill Inn

Troutbeck

Mrs Steele   Gill Head Farm, Troutbeck, nr Penrith,
                           Cumbria, CA11 0ST
Telephone/Fax   **017687 79652**
E-mail   **gillhead@talk21.com**
Rooms   3 double + 2 twin *(all en-suite)*
B&B   From £19.50-£20.00
Evening meal   £27.00
Packed lunch   £3.50 *(prior notice please)*
Distance from C2C   On route   Pub nearby

"Our comfortable 17th-c farmhouse set against the spectacular backdrop of Blencathra and the northern fells offers quality en-suite accommodation, log fires and delicious home cooking. Campsite with all facilites next door." **3 Diamonds.**
(See Advertisement on Page 79)

Mrs Maureen   Greenah Crag Farm, Troutbeck,
 Dix   nr Penrith, Cumbria CA11 0SQ
Telephone/fax   **01768483233**
Rooms   2 double + 1 twin *(en suite available)*
B&B   £16.50-£23.00
Packed lunch   £3.00 *(prior notice please)*
Distance from C2C   On route   Pub 3/4 mile

(No smoking please.) *"A warm welcome in our 17th-c farmhouse, central heating, tea/coffee-making facilities, TV lounge, bike lock-up."*

Greystoke

Mrs Jean Ashburner

	Lattendales Farm, Berrier Road, Greystoke, nr Penrith CA11 0UE
Telephone	**017684 83474**
Rooms	2 double + 1 twin
B&B	£17.00-£17.50
Distance from C2C	On route Pub nearby

(No smoking please.) "*17th-c farmhouse of character with comfortable accommodation well-recommended by cyclists. Interesting stone-built village with Greystoke Castle nearby.*"

Mrs Ann Cooper

	Meldene, Icold Road, Greystoke, nr Penrith, Cumbria CA11 0UG
Telephone/Fax	**017684 83856**
Rooms	1 double + 1 twin + 1 family
B&B	£16.50-£18.00 Packed lunch £3.50
Distance from C2C	On route Pub nearby

(No smoking please.) "*Detached family home near village centre. Tea/coffee-making facilities in all rooms. Clothes dried. Secure garage for cycles.*"

29

Greystoke

Mark
Thompson

	The Boot and Shoe Inn, Greystoke, nr Penrith, Cumbria CA11 0TP*
Telephone	**017684 83343**
Rooms	1 double + 2 twin + 1 family
B&B	£20.0-£25.00
Evening meal	Available 1900-2100hrs £5.50-£7.00
Packed lunch	£3.00 *(prior notice please)*
Distance from C2C	On route Pub

"An 18th-c coaching inn on main C2C route, situated in picturesque village of Greystoke." **(See advertisement on page 80)**

Mrs C Mole

	Brathen, The Thorpe, Greystoke, nr Penrith, Cumbria CA11 0TJ
Telephone/Fax	**017684 83595**
Rooms	3 double + 1 twin
B&B	£17.00
Packed lunch	£3.50
Distance from C2C	On route Pub 500 yds

"Converted barn on the outskirts of this quiet village. Comfortable accommodation and a hearty breakfast."

Mrs W. Theakston

	Orchard Cottage, Church Rd Greystoke nr Penrith, Cumbria
Telephone	**017684 83264 Fax 017684 80015**
E-mail	**wendy@theakstona.fsnet.co.uk**
Rooms	1 double + 1 family *(both en-suite)*
B&B	£22.00
Packed lunch	£3.50
Distance from C2C	On route Pub 100 yds

"Orchard Cottage offers warmth, comfort and good food with a safe lock up for cycles."

Motherby

Mrs Jackie Freeborn   Motherby House, Motherby,
                          nr Penrith, Cumbria CA11 0RS.
Telephone   **017684 83368**
e-mail   jacquie@enterprise.net
Rooms   2 family/twin   B&B   £17.00
Evening meal   £10.50 *(prior notice please)*
Packed lunch   £4.50 *(prior notice please)*
Distance from C2C   1 mile   Pub less than 1 mile

"An 18th-c house. Warm and friendly, beamed lounge, log fires, drying facilities, safe storage for bikes, and good food. Muddy bikers welcome!" **(See advertisement on page 80.)**

Blencowe

Barbara Fawcett   Little Blencowe Farm, Blencowe,
                      Penrith, Cumbria CA11 0DG
Telephone   **017684 83338 Fax 017684 83054**
e-mail   **bart.fawcett@ukgateway.net**
Rooms   1 family + 1 double + 1 twin
B&B   £17.50-£20.00
Packed lunch   £3.00
Distance from C2C   2 miles   Pub nearby

"Situated in a friendly village.   Comfortable Farm House accommodation with home cooking. Secure storage for bikes."

Newton Rigg

William O'Donovan Newton Rigg Campus, University of
Central Lancs. Penrith, Cumbria
CA11 0AH

Telephone	**01768 863791 Fax 01768 867249**
e-mail	**info@newtonrigg.ac.uk**
Rooms	230 singles! + 17 twins
B&B	From £18.00-£22.00
Evening meals	From £6.00 Packed lunch £3.50
Distance from C2C	On route Pub On site

Welcome Host. *"Standard & en-suite rooms. Meals available to non-residents. Secure cycle sheds. Bar. Shops. Laundrette."*

What is a Millennium Milepost?

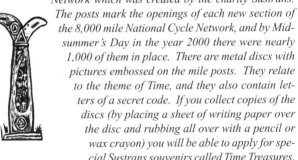

There are Millennium Mileposts along most of the National Cycle Network which was created by the charity Sustrans. The posts mark the openings of each new section of the 8,000 mile National Cycle Network, and by Mid-summer's Day in the year 2000 there were nearly 1,000 of them in place. There are metal discs with pictures embossed on the mile posts. They relate to the theme of Time, and they also contain letters of a secret code. If you collect copies of the discs (by placing a sheet of writing paper over the disc and rubbing all over with a pencil or wax crayon) you will be able to apply for special Sustrans souvenirs called Time Treasures. If you are really dedicated, you can go further and try to solve the secrets of the Time Trail Code!

If you want to know more information about the Time Trail please write to Sustrans PO Box 21 Bristol BS99 2HA or 'phone 0117 929 0888

PENRITH

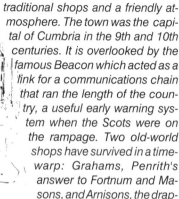

Known locally as the Red Town because of its sandstone buildings, Penrith is a picturesque market town with traditional shops and a friendly atmosphere. The town was the capital of Cumbria in the 9th and 10th centuries. It is overlooked by the famous Beacon which acted as a link for a communications chain that ran the length of the country, a useful early warning system when the Scots were on the rampage. Two old-world shops have survived in a time-warp: Grahams, Penrith's answer to Fortnum and Masons, and Arnisons, the drapers, established in 1740 and once the home of Wordworth's grandparents.

Until the end of the 14th-c the town had no water supply. In 1385 Bishop Strickland diverted Thacka Beck from the river Peterill and an environmentally aware agreement allowed the townspeople to draw daily only as much water from the Peterill as would flow through the eye of a millstone.
You can see the millstone outside the Tourist Information Centre.

Penrith Castle dates from the 15th-c when an existing pele tower was crenellated. The area would certainly have witnessed some violent times from across the Borders in the past.

33

Penrith Tourist Information

PLACES OF INTEREST

Robinson's School Middlegate: TIC and Museum. Local history on show and regular exhibitions

St Andrew's Church The Giant's Grave in the Churchyard: legendary slayer of monsters from Inglewood Forest!

EATING OUT

The Narrowgate Coffee Shop The Narrows: best coffee in town 01768 862599

The Bewick Princes Street 01768 864764

A Taste of Bengal Stricklandgate **01768 891700**

Bit on the Side Brunswick Square 01768 892526

CYCLE SHOPS

Arragons' Brunswick Road 01768 890344 **(see advertisement on page 81)**

Harpers Cycles 1-2 Middlegate 01768 864475

C2C Route Features: the Watermill at Little Salkeld, organic millers with art gallery and café. Long Meg and her Daughters, a pre-historic stone circle (don't dance on the Sabbath, you may be turned into one of these stones!). If you go through Melmerby don't miss the famous Village Bakery and the Shepherds Inn.

Long Meg and her Daughters

Penrith

Julie & Mike Davidson	Glendale, 4 Portland Place, Penrith, Cumbria CA11 7QN
Telephone	**01768 862579 Fax 01768 867934**
e-mail	**glendale@lineone.net**
Rooms	1 single + 4 twin + 2 double +4 family
B&B	£16.00- £26.00 Packed lunch £3.50
Distance from C2C	On route Restaurant nearby

"**Three Diamonds.** *Spacious house with friendly comfortable atmosphere. After a good night's rest the famous Glendale breakfast will set you up for the climb to Alston and beyond!.*"

Eileen Reid and Peter Sowerby	Brandelhow Guest House, 1 Portland Place, Penrith, Cumbria CA11 7QW
Telephone	**01768 864470**
Rooms	1 single + 4 double/twin + 1 family
B&B	£17.50-£21.50
Packed lunch	£3.75 *(prior notice please)*
Distance from C2C	On route Pub nearby

3 Diamonds ETB. *"Victorian town house on C2C route. Comfortable beds and a good English breakfast for the weary cyclist! Tea/coffee, colour TV, washing and drying facilities."*

Kim Mawer	Corney House, 1Corney Place, Penrith, Cumbria CA11 7PY
Telephone	**01768 867627**
e-mail	kimrose@talk21.com
Bunkhouse Style	6 beds (mixed sex)
B&B	£10.00 - £12.00 On C2C route
Evening meal	From £5.00 Packed lunch £3.00

Breakfast not included-can be requested

"*Unique bunkhouse provides friendly hostel accommodation. Close to excellent pub, cinema, takeaways, restaurants. Home made organic food on request. Kitchen available for self catering. Drying facilities.*"

Penrith

Mr and	Woodland House Hotel,
Mrs Davies	Wordsworth Street, Penrith, CA11 7QY
Telephone	**01768 864177** Fax 01768 890152
e-mail	davies@woodlandhouse.co.uk.
Website	www.woodlandhouse.co.uk
Rooms	2 double + 3 single + *2 twins + 1 family* (all en-suite)
B&B	£24.00-£29.50
Packed lunch	£3.50 *(prior notice please)*
Distance from C2C	On route Pub nearby

(No smoking please.) **3 diamonds.** *"Elegant, spacious licensed private hotel at the bottom of Beacon Hill, tea/coffee-making facilities, colour TV. Library of tourist information."*

Sylvia Jackson	Norcroft Guest House,Graham Street Penrith, Cumbria CA11 9LQ
Telephone/Fax	**01768 862365**
Rooms	3 family + 3 double + 2 twin +1 single
B&B	£15.00-£24.50
Evening meal	£5.50 *(prior notice please)*
Packed Lunch	£3.50
Distance from C2C	On route Pub nearby

4 Diamonds Commended *warm welcome award* *"Large Victorian house, comfortable rooms, mostly en-suite, tea/coffee-making facilities, colour TV, drying facilities, secure cycle storage."***(See Advertisement on Page 82)**

Penrith

Mr Graham Carruthers	Roundthorn Country House, Beacon Edge, Penrith, CA11 8SJ
Telephone	**01768 863952 Fax 01768 864100**
e-mail	**enquiries@roundthorn.fsnet.co.uk**
Rooms	1 twin + 8 doubles +1 family
B&B	£25.00-£32.50 Packed lunch £3.50
Distance from C2C	On route Pub 1 mile (*hotel has bar*)

3 Diamonds *silver award* "*A beautiful Georgian mansion with spectacular views. All rooms en-suite, licensed bar, washing and drying facilities and a hearty Cumbrian breakfast.*"

Gregor & Joanne Land	Caledonia Guest House, 8 Victoria Rd Penrith, CA11 8HR
Telephone	**01768 864482**
e-mail	**greg.land@virgin.net**
Rooms	3 twin + 2 doubles +1 family
B&B	£16.00-£20.00 Packed lunch £3.00
Distance from C2C	On route Pub 1 mile

"*Comfortable Victorian town house offering all bedrooms with en-suite or private bathrooms. All rooms have tea/coffee making facilities. Ideal location for C2C.*"

Debbie & Leon Kirk	Brooklands Guest House, 2 Portland Place, Penrith, CA11 7QN
Telephone	**01768 863395 Fax 01768 864895**
Rooms	2 singles + 3 twin + 2 doubles+1family
B&B	£18.00 Packed lunch £3.50
Distance from C2C	On route Pub 1 mile

"*A fine Victorian town house just 100m from the town centre. Luxury en-suite rooms available with all facilities. Very secure storage for cycles.*"

Penrith

Jim & Margaret Hodge

	Agricultural Hotel, Castlegate, Penrith, Cumbria CA11 7JE
Telephone	**01768 862622**
Rooms	1 twin + 1 double +2 family
B&B	£20.00 - £40.00 Packed lunch £4.00
Evening meal	Yes
Distance from C2C	On route

"A traditional country pub in the town with log fires, a warm welcome, good accommodation, home made food. 5 Traditional cask ales and secure bike storage."

Mrs Blundell

	Albany House, 5 Portland Place, Penrith, Cumbria CA11 7QN
Telephone/Fax	**01768 863072**
Rooms	4 family (sleeps 5) + 1 double
B&B	From £17.50 Packed lunch £3.75
Distance from C2C	On route Pub nearby

3 Diamonds ETB. *"Mid-Victorian town house, spacious comfortable rooms, tea/coffee, colour/satellite TV, free clothes drying, secure indoor storage for cycles."*

Barbara & Dave Hughes

	Blue Swallow Guest House, 11 Victoria Road, Penrith, CA11 8HR
Telephone/Fax	**01768 866335**
Rooms	5 twin + 3 doubles +3 family
B&B	£17.00-£20.00 Packed lunch £3.50
Distance from C2C	On route Restaurants nearby

3 Diamonds *"A fine Victorian town house on edge of town centre. Very clean, comforable rooms mostly en-suite. Good hearty breakfast and lock up for parking cycles."*

Edenhall

The Proprietor	The Country Hotel, Edenhall, nr Penrith, Cumbria CA11 8SX.
Telephone	**01768 881454** Fax 01768 881266
Rooms	4 double + 6 single + 10 twins 4 family rooms *(all en-suite)*
B&B	£25.00
Evening meal	From £5.50 Packed lunch £3.95
Distance from C2C	On route Hotel has Public Bar

2 Diamond Hotel. *"Country house hotel in beautiful surroundings. TV, telephone, tea/coffee in all rooms. Excellent food. Secure cycle storage and drying facilities. Telephone for brochure."*

Langwathby

Clive Gravett	Langstanes, Culgaith Road, Langwathby, nr Penrith CA10 1NA
Telephone/Fax	**01768 881004**
Rooms	2 double + 1 twin *(all en-suite)*
B&B	£21.00 Packed lunch from £3.50
Distance from C2C	On route Pub 300 yds

(No smoking please.) **ETB 4 Diamonds** *"Comfortable sandstone house on route, tea/coffee-making facilities, colour TV, secure bike storage, drying facilities."*

Mrs Karen Peet	Hayloft Bunkhouse, Langwathby Hall Farm, Langwathby, Penrith, CA10 1LW
Telephone	**01768 881771** Fax 01768 881802
Rooms	36 bunks (2 cubicles of 8 + 2 of 10)
B&B	£14.00 *(Full English breakfast)*
Packed lunch	£3.50
Distance from C2C	On route Pub 150 yds

(No smoking please.) *"Very comfortable bunkhouse accommodation in converted stable loft, with hot showers, and breakfast served in the farmhouse. Eden Ostrich World."*

Langwathby

Nancy Atkinson	Bank House Farm and Stables, Little Salkeld, Langwathby, Cumbria CA10 INN
Telephone/fax	**01768 881257**
Rooms	3 doubles + 3 family + 3 twins
B&B	£20.00-£30.00
Packed lunch	£3.95
Distance from C2C	On route
Pub	1 mile

"B&B or self-catering in converted barns and farm cottages for individuals, families or larger groups. Secure cycle storage and a warm friendly family welcome awaits" (**See Advertisement page 82.**)

Renwick

Mr and Mrs Milburn	Half Way Bunk House, Busk Rigg, Renwick, nr Penrith, Cumbria CA10 1LA. *(£40.00 per bunk room)*
Telephone	**01768 898288 or 897155**
Rooms	2 rooms, 6 bunks each, £8.00 *(sleeping bags available-please phone)*
Evening meal	By arrangement Packed lunch £3.50
Distance from C2C	½ mile Pub 3½ miles

"Located in the hamlet of Busk on working farm. Kitchen with

hob, microwave oven, toaster and fridge. Storage heating, shower, toilets, dining and sitting area - lift to pub available."

Melmerby

*This delightful village is 3 miles off the route but is well worth the visit as it has so much to offer and lots of facilities. The **Village Bakery** has a coffee shop and restaurant. It is famous for excellent home baking. **The Shepherds Inn** is renowned for its delicious puddings and its Egon Ronay Listing.*

Thomas and Margaret Frazer	Bolton Farmhouse, Melmerby, nr Penrith, Cumbria CA10 1HF
Telephone	**01768 881851 Mobile 0402 933 952**
Rooms	1 single + 1 double + 1 twin
B&B	£16.00 Distance from C2C 3 miles

"17th-c farmhouse, centrally situated, in an area of outstanding natural beauty. wonderful views, open fires, comfortable and friendly. Nearby pub, serves good food. All welcome."

Mrs Edith James	Greenholme, Melmerby, nr Penrith, Cumbria CA10 1HB
Telephone	**01768 881436**
Web	www.erudite.co.uk/greenholme
Rooms	1 double + 1 double with extra bed + 1 double with extra bed en-suite
B&B	From £18.00-£20.00
Distance from C2C	on alternative route Pub nearby

(No smoking please.) "Comfortable accommodation for the weary cyclist. All rooms have tea/coffee-making facilities. A good English breakfast before the big climb up Hartside."

ALSTON

Market Square

A picture postcard Cumbrian market town hidden away in England's last wilderness. Cobbled streets wind steeply up to the old market square where you will find quaint old cafés and shops. This historic town, built on the confluence of the South Tyne and the river Nent, owes much to the lead-mining heritage of the area. The mines and their machinery are silent now, but scattered hill farms where mining families grew crops to subsidise their meagre wages and the haunting sound of the curlew still remain. Once you visit this area, its beauty and history will lure you back to explore more of its secrets.

South Tynedale Railway

Alston Tourist Information

PLACES OF INTEREST

Hartside Nursery Garden	On route 1 mile from Alston: rare and unusual alpine plants
South Tynedale Railway	TIC and beautifully restored Victorian station, England's highest narrow-gauge railway 01434 381696

EATING OUT

Gossipgate Gallery	The Butts, back of the old market: tea room and craft gallery 01434 381806
The Angel	Town Centre 01434 381363
Lowbyer Manor	Excellent food - Main course £9.50 Mrs Hughes 01434 381230

*C2C Route Features: Don't miss this unique market town set amidst the wildrness of the Pennines. The route officialy goes through Leadgate and thence to Garrigill and Nenthead. Garrigill has a post office and pub. Nenthead has a newly opened **Mines Heritage Centre**, a pub, a cafè and village shop. If you take the Stanhope route, **Killhope Lead mining Centre** is excellent.*

WARNING! This area is in a very remote corner of the UK: places to buy food or stay over-night are few and far between.

Alston Moor

Leadgate

Mike and Clare Le Marie	Brownside House, Leadgate, Alston, Cumbria CA9 3EL
Telephone	**Fax/phone 01434 382169**
	Phone 01434 382100
e-mail	brownside_hse@hotmail.com
Rooms	1 double + 2 twin + 1 single
B&B	£18.00
Evening meal	£6.50 Packed lunch £2.50
Distance from C2C	On route Pub 2 miles

3 Diamonds *"Quiet, peaceful situation in the country with a warm welcome. Home cooking, hot bath. Residents' lounge with TV and log fire. Secure storage for bikes."*

Alston

Mr and Mrs P.J. & M. Hughes	Lowbyer Manor Country House Hotel, Alston, Cumbria CA9 3JX
Telephone	**01434 381230** Fax 01434 382937
Web site	**www.lowbyemanor.ntb.org.uk**
Rooms	6 double + 2 single + 4 twins + 1 family
B&B	£29.50 *(all rooms en-suite)*
Dinner (à la carte)	From £9.50 Packed lunch from £3.50
Distance from C2C	On alternative route Pub nearby

2 Star Hotel *"17th-c comfortable family-run manor, substantial breakfast and a la carte dinner. In quiet wooded location on edge of Alston. Drying facilities available. Secure garage for bikes."*

Alston

Adam Ferguson	St Paul's Mission, Town Head, Alston, Cumbria CA9 3SL*
Telephone/Fax	**01434 382441**
Rooms	36 bed-cubicled accommodation
B&B	£10.00-£15.00
Distance from C2C	On alternative route Pub nearby

(No smoking please.) "100 yds from Market Square, 8 showers and W.C.s, indoor bike security, sauna, large lounge, Sky TV, cooking , launderette, full central heating, large garden."

C. Sorrell	Blueberry's Guesthouse and Restaurant, Market Pl, Alston CA9 3QN
Telephone	**01434 381928**
Rooms	1 double + 1 twin + 1 family
B&B	£17.50-£20.00
Evening meal	From £5.00-£6.00 Packed lunch £3.50
Distance from C2C	On alternative route Pub nearby

(No smoking in bedrooms please.) **Commended.** *"Queen Anne Grade II listed town house, 25 yds from shops and pubs. Comfortable bedrooms with hospitality tray & TV. Full Cumbrian breakfast, under-cover cycle store."*

Alston

David & Alison Hymers	The Cumberland Hotel, Town Foot, Alston, Cumbria CA9 3HX
Telephone	**01434 381875 Fax 01434 382035**
Rooms	3 doubles + 2 twins + 3 family
B&B	£22.00-£26.00
Evening Meal	From £5.00-£15.00 Pk. lunch £3.50
Distance from C2C	On alternative route Pub nearby

"All rooms en-suite, bike storage, drying/cleaning facilities. Only stamping point in Alston. Choice of traditional cask ales & home cooked food. Family run."

Mrs Coleman	Albert House Guesthouse,Townhead, Alston, Cumbria CA9 3SL
Telephone/fax	**01434 381793**
E-mail	**albert.house.@amserve.net**
Rooms	2 double + 3 twin + 2 family + 3 single
B&B	£20.00-£25.00
Evening meal	£5.00-£12.00 Packed lunch £3.50
Distance from C2C	On alternative route Pub nearby

*(No smoking please.)***ETB 3 diamonds** *"After a hard day in the saddle enjoy the luxury of Albert House. Warm and friendly. Excellent evening meals. Large Cumbrian breakfast and substantial packed lunches."*

Steve & Tian Smith	Victoria Inn, Front Street, Alston, Cumbria CA9 3SE
Telephone/Fax	**01434 381194**
e-mail	**victoriainncumbria@talk21.com**
Rooms	3 single + 3 double + 2 family
B&B	£14.50-£18.00
Distance from C2C	On alternative route Pub: in house

"Friendly family run town inn/B&B. Fine beers, bar & restaurant meals (Chinese & Indian speciality) C2C, bikers and walkers welcome."

GARRIGILL

This peaceful little village was once a bustling lead mining community. In 1831 the population was 1,614, today it is a mere 225. The rounded hillocks around the village betray the sites of lead mine workings, many of them tree covered, but in the mining heyday not a tree was to be seen between Nenthead and Alston. Garrigill has a pub and a post office, and some guest houses do excellent evening meals. You may be interested to visit **Pennine Llama Treks** *at Ivy House.*

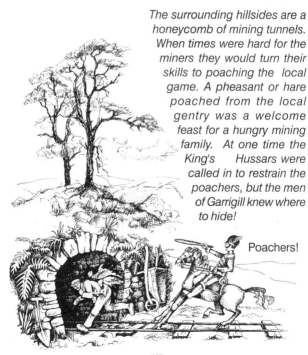

The surrounding hillsides are a honeycomb of mining tunnels. When times were hard for the miners they would turn their skills to poaching the local game. A pheasant or hare poached from the local gentry was a welcome feast for a hungry mining family. At one time the King's Hussars were called in to restrain the poachers, but the men of Garrigill knew where to hide!

Poachers!

47

Garrigill

Mrs Pauline Platts
(on B6277)

High Windy Hall Hotel & Restaurant,
Above Garrigill, Alston, CA9 3EZ

Telephone	**01434 381547**
Fax	**01434 382477**
e-mail	sales@hwh.u-net.com
Web site	www.hwh.u-net.com
Rooms	2 double + 1 twin + 2 family *(all en-suite)*
B&B	£27.50-£35.00
Evening meal	From £17.00-£21.50
Packed lunch	£3.50
Distance from C2C	200 metres
Pub	½ mile

(No smoking in bedrooms please.) **ETB 4 Diamonds.** *"Family-run licensed hotel, good food, interesting wine list, peaceful views overlooking South Tyne Valley, well-deserved luxury after Hartside Pass."*

Lead Mining

Garrigill

Anne Bramwell

	Post Office Guest House, Garrigill, Alston, Cumbria CA9 3DS
Telephone/Fax	**01434 381257/Fax 01434 381257**
Rooms	1 double + 2 twin + 2 singles
B&B	£17.00 Packed lunch £3.50
Distance from C2C	On route Pub nearby

(No smoking please.) "*The Post Office is a 300 year old house. Tea/coffee-making facilities, radio alarms and hair dryers in all rooms, separate residents' lounge with TV. Drying facilities available. Good food at pub next door.*"

Mrs Laurie Humble

	Ivy House B&B, Garrigill, Alston, Cumbria CA9 3DU
Telephone/Fax	**01434 382501/Fax 01434 382660**
e-mail	ivyhouse@garrigill.com
Web site:	www.garrigill.com
Rooms	3 double/twin + 2 family
	3 singles - *(all en-suite)*
B&B	£18.50-£29.00
Evening meal	£8.00-£15.00 *(book ahead please)*
Packed lunch	£4.00
Distance from C2C	On route Pub: Nearby

(No smoking please.)
ETB 4 Diamonds & AA

"*Converted 17th-c farmhouse. Comfortable en-suite rooms with TVs. Residents' lounge with TV. Secure cycle storage. Cycle cleaning facilities. Laundry service. CTC affiliated. Friendly hosts!*".

NENTHEAD

Nenthead from Garrigill Road

Nestling in the bowl of its surrounding hills, Nenthead is one of the highest villages in England. It was the most important lead-mining centre in the North Pennines from the beginning of 18th-c. Lead was probably discovered very early by accident when local farmers used fire to crack the stone in order to build walls around their land. It was found that a substance in the rock melted and could be formed into useful vessels. Much later they realised that the lead had great commercial value and small drift mines were opened.

The Quaker run London Lead Mining Company contributed enormously to the welfare of all the local inhabitants as well as the miners. The Company gradually provided Nenthead with all the social services such as schools, chapels, shops, a reading room, village hall and houses. The 'Miners Arms' regularly had its rent reduced as trade diminished due to the miners "preferring books to beer"!

Nenthead Tourist Information

PLACES OF INTEREST

Mines Heritage Centre   Excellent exhibition and exciting underground experience in newly restored Lead Mine-don't miss! Also very good cafe attached to The Heritage Centre.

EATING OUT

The Crown Inn   Has a paddock at back for campers (please put donation in box!) 01434 381271

The Miners Arms   Bunk House   01434 381427

Mines Heritage Centre Café   Good homemade food.01434 382037

BIKE REPAIRS

Mark Fearn   Blacksmith - repairs bikes & carries some spares. Phone **01434 382194**
Bike & rider recovery where possible

Carting lead

Nenthead

Janet Cresswell Mill Cottage Bunkhouse, Nenthead,
Alston, Cumbria CA9 3PD

Telephone	**01434 382726** Fax 382294	
e-mail	administration.office@virgin.net	
Bunkhouse	Sleeps 9	Bed only £8.00
B&B	£12.00	Packed lunch £3.50
Distance from C2C	On route	Pub nearby

"Superior quality bunkhouse accommodation. Right on C2C route. Set amidst spectacular scenery. Washing/drying facilities. Fully fitted kitchen. Secure cycle storage."

The Miners Arms Nenthead, Alston, Cumbria CA9 3PF

Telephone	**01434 381427**	
e-mail	miners.arms@talk21.com	
Rooms	2 double, 2 family, 2 twin, 2 single	
B&B	£15.00	
Bunkhouse	Sleeps 12	B&B £10.00
Evening meals	From £4.00	Packed lunch £3.25
Distance from C2C	On route	Stamping Post

(No smoking in bedrooms or bunkhouse please.) *"Friendly family pub offering homely accommodation.National prize-winning menu. Home-made food and real ale. Bike spares available."*

Allendale

The Dale Hotel Market Place, Allendale, NE47 9BD

Telephone	**01434 683212**	
Reservations	**01207 235354**	
Rooms	9 double, 3 family, 12 twin, 6 single	
B&B	£22.00-£39.00 *(Group discounts)*	
Evening meals	Available	Packed lunch £3.25
Distance from C2C	8 miles	

"Comfortable country hotel with a variety of bedrooms to suit individual requirements. Hearty breakfast, buffet and sauna."

ALLENHEADS

Allenheads, reputed to be England's highest village, would have looked very different 100 years ago. A valley filled with toneless grey slag heaps and shrouded by the smog from miners' cottage fires would have greeted you. Today this friendly little hamlet, almost hidden in pine trees, welcomes you off the moor with its babbling beck and good places to eat and rest. Allenheads once supplied a sixth of Britain's lead until cheap foreign imports brought tumbling prices and an end to the village's mining prosperity.

PLACES OF INTEREST

Heritage Centre	*In the midst of the village.*
Old School House	*Art Exhibitions.*
Old Blacksmith's Shop	*Displays of local items.*

PLACES TO EAT

The Henmel Café	*Welcoming oasis for the tired, wet and hungry cyclist.*
Allenheads Inn	*A warm welcome & good food*
Old School House	*Fresh, delicious hearty home cooking*
The Village Shop	*Has a good supply of food as well as basic essentials for your bike.*

Allenheads

Peter & Linda Stenson

The Allenheads Inn, Allenheads, Hexham, Northumberland NE47 9HJ

Telephone/Fax **01434 685200**

Rooms 4 double + 4 twin + 3 family *(en-suite)* (cottage for groups)

B&B £21.50-£25.00

Evening meal From £5.00

Distance from C2C On route *(Pub has smoking & non bars)*

"Well renowned reputation. A must for many cyclists who enjoy the atmosphere, hospitality and all round comfort. Fine ales and huge helpings of tasty food!" **(See advertisement on page 83)**

Helen Ratcliffe and Alan Smith

The Old School House, Allenheads, Northumberland NE47 9HR

Telephone/Fax **01434 685040**

e-mail headalan@aol.com

Rooms 1 family room (sleeps 1-4) Bunk-bed room for larger groups *Linen provided*

B&B £16.00-£18.00

Evening meal Available

Distance from C2C On route   Pub nearby

"A friendly, colourful and interesting place. Superb dinner and tremendous breakfast, best so far on route. Great atmosphere, unrivalled views. Altogether a wonderful place to stay!" (Quotes from C2C'ers)

Allenheads

The AllenheadsTrust,
Allenheads Heritage Centre, Allenheads,
Northumberland NE47 9UQ.
Telephone **01434 685043**
Fax 01434 685043
(Advertisement on page 85)

Pat & Terry McMullon	New Houses, Allenheads, Northumberland NE47 9HX
Telephone	**01434 685260 Fax 01434 685260**
e-mail	**petermcmullon@hotmnail.com**
Rooms	1 single + 1 double + 1 twin
B&B	£20.00
Evening meal	From £9.00 Packed lunch £3.50
Distance from C2C	On route Pub Nearby

" *'New Houses' was new in 1788! today it is a warm, spacious and very comfortable cottage with all amenities.* "

ROOKHOPE

This little-visited settlement welcomes you after a glorious two miles free-wheel ride from the last summit. Rookhope keeps the secret of its hiding place well guarded as it nestles far from sight high above the Weardale Valley. It is hard to imagine that this small group of dwellings was a hive of activity only a few

years ago. In its heyday it supported a surgery, a resident district nurse, vicar, policeman, teashops, several crowded pubs and a busy school. The mining of lead, iron and fluorspar, smelting and the railways totally dominated people's lives with clockwork regularity. Today the village is a welcome watering hole and resting place for weary cyclists before the final leg of the C2C journey down to the NE coast.

There is an information centre at Rookhope Nurseries, and a pub, village shop and several guest-houses.

Rookhope

Lintzgarth Arch

Lintzgarth Arch stands enormous, abandoned and out of place on the valley floor on the approach to Rookhope. The arch carried a horizontal chimney across the valley which replaced the more conventional vertical type when it was realised that a lot of lead literally went up with the smoke. Consequently young chimney sweepswere employed to scrape the valuable lead and silver deposits from the chimney once a week. A dangerous job done by young- sters long before the days of Health and Safety!

Broken flue and chimney

Rookhope

Janette and Tony Newbon	High Brandon, Rookhope, Weardale, Co. Durham, DL13 2AF
Telephone	**01388 517673**
e-mail	**highbrandonbb@aol.com**
Web site:	**http://members.aol.com/highbrandonbb**
Rooms	1 double + 1 twin + 1 family *(all en-suite)*
B&B	From £17.00-£25.00
Evening Meal	£5.50-£10.50 Packed lunch £3.00
Distance from C2C	On route Pub 1 mile

4 Diamonds (No smoking please.) "A superior restored, atmospheric farmhouse, magnificent panoramic views, original features. Excellent food/en-suite accommodation, guest lounge, warm welcome. Highly regarded by cyclists worldwide. Larger parties catered for."

Mike and Kay Leathers	Garden Cottage Guest House, 7 Front Street, Rookhope, Bishop Auckland DL13 2AZ
Telephone	**01388 517577**
Rooms	1 double + 1 twin + 1 family + 1 single
B&B	£16.00-£20.00
Evening meal	£6.00 Packed lunch £3.00
Distance from C2C	On route Pub nearby

(No smoking in bedrooms please.) "Stone-built cottage with beamed ceilings, open fires, guests' lounge, TV and tea/coffee in bedrooms, drying facilities, garage for bikes. Great food, warm welcome."

58

Rookhope

Colin & Pauline Lomas	The Old Vicarage, Rookhope in Weardale, Co. Durham, DL13 2AF
Telephone/fax	**01388 517375**
Rooms	1 single + 1 double
B&B	£17.50
Evening Meal	£7.50 Packed lunch £3.50
Distance from C2C	On route Pub *(lift available)*

(Large detached, stone-built house in own secluded grounds. Spacious room with tea and coffee-making facilities. TV + video, garage for bikes and drying facilities. Resident dog. Camping in the garden available.

Weardale

Mrs J.S. Robinson	Dales Farm, Copt Hill, Cowshill, Weardale, Co. Durham, DL13 1AD
Telephone	**01388 537400**
Rooms	1 twin + 1 double
B&B	£17.00
Evening Meal	£8.00 Packed lunch £3.50
Distance from C2C	3 miles Pub *(lift available)*

"A friendly welcome and comfortable farmhouse accommodation. Four poster double bed. Tea/coffee making facilities. Clothes dried. Locked garage for bikes available."

STANHOPE

You may wish to cycle via Stanhope, an attractive Weardale village nestling between the Northern Dales. The village expanded in 1845 when the Stanhope & Tyne Railway was constructed. A standing engine hauled the heavy wagons up Crawley Side. It then continued on its journey down the Waskerley Way to Consett and Cleveland.

PLACES OF INTEREST

Dales Visitor Centre	Town centre 01388 527650 Good cafe too.
Fossil tree at St Thomas's Church	350 million years old, found in 1914 in an Edmundbyers mine

EATING OUT

Stanhope Old Hall	A la carte menu 01388 528 451
The Bike Stop	Stamping post & great teas. Mile post 100
Waskerley Tea Rooms	Margaret's wonderful teas at mile post 106
Various pubs	All in town centre

CYCLE SHOPS

Weardale Mountain Bikes	Frosterley 01388 528129 (within 5 miles of C2C)

*C2C Features: the route leads you up Crawley Side, aptly named due to its steep incline, and on up to the **Waskerley Way**. Before the railways were built, all raw materials were transported by pack horses. Teams of tough little Galloway horses would pick their way across the wind-swept Pennines and then down into the valleys. The lead horse often had a bell attached to his harness to guide the following horses across the mist-cloaked moors.*

Stanhope

Mrs. Storey   Queen's Head Hotel, 89 Front Street,
Stanhope, Weardale DL13 2UB

Telephone	**01388 528160**
Rooms	4 twins
B&B	£20.00
Evening meal	From £3.00
Packed lunch	£3.00
Distance from C2C	c. 1 mile Hotel has Public Bar

"Small family-run country pub, full licence, fine real ales & good food. All rooms have colour TV and tea/coffee-making facilities."

Mrs E. Hamilton   Red Lodge Guest House, 2 Market
Place, Stanhope, DL13 2UN

Telephone	**01388 527851**
e-mail	redlodge@netline.uk.net
Rooms	1 double + 1 twin + 1 family +1 single
B&B	£20.00-£22.50
Distance from C2C	c.1 mile Pub nearby

"Family run guest-house, well-equipped with TV and tea/coffee-making facilities in all rooms. Pubs and fast food takeaways nearby. Quote from visitor's book 1999 : 'Weary cyclist's rating - Bed 5 Star, Welcome 5 Star & Food 5 Star!' "

 Terry & Lorraine Turnbull "The Bike Stop" Parkhead Station. Official NCN Stamping Station. *"An ongoing development of converting the former Station Master's House to Tea Rooms and B&B specifically designed for the sustainable traveller. C2C merchandise, refreshments, WC, telephone, bicycle spares, local information and a warm welcome."*

Location: On C2C - *(Mile point 100)*
Tel/Fax: **01388 526434**

CONSETT

As the C2C approaches Consett it passes the site of the Old Consett Steel Works which originally opened in 1837. It was eventually closed and the enormous site was dismantled in 1980. This ghost-like empty space of 700 acres now looks strange and desolate after those Dickensian years when the night skies glowed bright with fires from hungry steel blast-furnaces.

PLACES OF INTEREST

Phileas Fogg Factory	Alias Derwent Valley Foods
Shotley Bridge	An old spa town, well-known for German sword-makers in the 17th-c

EATING OUT

Grey Horse	Real Ales brewed on the premises! Light lunches and right on C2C route.
Fountain Pub	Madomsley Road. 2 mins. from C2C(by Safeways.)Sandwiches.Restaurant & flask filling service. Friendly welcome to C2Cers. Phone Maureen.01207 502765
Jolly Drovers Pub	Leadgate 01207 503 994

CYCLE SHOPS

Consett Cycle Co	62 Medomsley Rd 01207 581 205
McVickers Sports	Front Street 01207 505 121

C2C Features: *dotted along the line are story-boards set on vertical sleepers which interpret the history of the railway. These are chapters taken from a novel,* The Celestial Railroad, *by John Downie. It is available from Sustrans North Eastern Office at Stanley, 01207 281259.*

Castleside

Liz Lawson   Bee Cottage Farm, Castleside,
                  Consett, Co. Durham DH8 9HW
Telephone   **01207 508224**
Rooms   3 double + 3 twins + 4 family + 1 single
B&B   From £22.00-£35.00 On C2C route
Evening meal   £14.50   Packed lunch £5.00
(No smoking please.) **ETB 3 Diamonds**

"Working farm with lovely views, situated close to the Waskerley Way (between points 105 and 106 on C2C map). Sleeps 34. Warm welcome, home comforts, ***good food and plenty of it****! Tearoom open 1pm-6pm all summer."* ***(See Page 84.)***

Noel and Jane Castleside Inn, Staniford-Dam, Consett,
   Reid   Co. Durham DH8 8EP.
Telephone   **01207 581443**   Fax 01207 583373
Internet   http://www.scoot.co.uk/castleside
Rooms   1 single + 4 double + 2 twin + 1 family
B&B   £17.95-£26.95 *(10% discount for C2C)*
Meals available   11.00am-10.30pm Public Bar
Packed lunch   Available   On C2C Route
"Rural setting very near C2C route. Carry on over A68. Turn left after viaduct by old coal wagon! Quality accommodation, all en-suite."

Castleside

Margaret Wigham	Greenside Farm, Waskerley, Castleside, Consett, Co. Durham DH8 9DR
Telephone	**01207 509663**
Rooms	1 single + 1 family
B&B	From £13.00 On C2C route
Evening meal	From £8.00 Packed lunch £3.00

"Small holding directly on C2C. Wholesome home cooking by professional cook. Wonderful views. Lovely garden and a warm welcome to all."

Mr Gordon Sanderson	Deneview, 15 Front street, Castleside, Consett, Co. Durham DH8 9AR
Telephone	**01207 502925**
E-mail	**cyndyglancy@lineone.net**
Rooms	2 double + 1 twin
B&B	From £18.00-£22.00 On C2C route
Evening meal	Yes Packed lunch £3.00

*(No smoking please.)*3 Diamonds *"Friendly, superior accommodation with en-suite rooms. TV/tea & coffee, secure bike storage and a hearty breakfast to set you on your way!"*

Consett

David Hodgson	Consett YMCA, Parliament Street, Consett, Co. Durham DH8 5DH
Telephone	**01207 502680** Fax **01207 501578**
E-mail	**ymca@derwentside.org.net**
Rooms	12 family rooms Pub nearby
B&B	£12.50 Evening meal £5.00
Distance from C2C	Very near Packed lunch £3.00

"We have a drying room, workshop for repairs, colour TV, bar and lounge, table tennis and pool table, roller-blade disco and a gym if you have the energy left!" **(See advertisement on page 83.)**

STANLEY

Stanley is set on a breezy hill top and commands a bird's eye view of the whole area. **Sustrans North Eastern Office** *is at Rockwood House, Barn Hill, Stanley, Co. Durham DH9 8AN. Tel: 01207 281259, Fax 01207 281113. Information on other Sustrans Bike Routes is available here together with interesting booklets and C2C T-shirts. You may join the Sustrans Charity here. They are responsible for creating a UK cycle-way network.*

PLACES OF INTEREST

Tanfield Railway	World's oldest operating railway!
Beamish	Open-air museum

EATING OUT

Hill Top Restaurant	East Street 01207 233217
Asda	On ring road, Coffee Shop
Shafto's Bar	Causey Farm 01207 235555

CYCLE SHOPS

MainBrothersFront Street
01207 290258

***Features*: *Beamish Museum* *is England's largest open-air museum and has a working steam railway, trams, a Victorian town centre, a demonstration colliery, a school and a working farm. The C2C route passes within yards of the entrance gate.*

Scene from Beamish Museum

65

Stanley

Mrs B Fraser

	Hedley Hall, Hedley Lane, Nr.Sunniside Stanley, Newcastle-on-Tyne NE16 5EH
Telephone	**01207 231835**
e-mail	**hedleyhall@aol.com**
Rooms	1 double + 1 twin + 1 single + 1 family
B&B	£25.00-£30.00
Distance from C2C	2 miles (behind Beamish Museum)
Pub	½ mile (happy to provide lifts)

4 Diamonds. *"An attractive georgian house set in 7 acres, overlooking the Museum, panoramic views, tranquil setting facilities in all rooms. Close to Beamish Museum."*

Beamish

Clare Jones

	Beamish Mary Inn, No Place, Beamish, Co. Durham DH9 0QH
Telephone	**0191 370 0237** Fax 0191 370 0091
Rooms	3 double + 1 family (all en-suite)
B&B	£20.00-£25.00
Evening meal	From £4.00
Distance from C2C	¼ mile
Pub	Nearby

3 Diamonds *"Traditional Inn. Specialises in good food, real ale, live music. Comfortable atmosphere. All rooms en-suite, 1 with bath. (Landlord and landlady both keen cyclists.)"*

CHESTER-LE-STREET

Chester-le-Street is the oldest town in County Durham, and was once a Roman settlement. The Washington Wildfowl and Wetlands Centre is very near the route. This 100-acre waterfowl park designed by Peter Scott has over 1,200 birds and is visited by several mammals including the scarce water vole.

PLACES OF INTEREST

The Washington 100 acres of magnificent parkland, ponds
  Wetlands Trust and hides 0191 416 5454

EATING OUT

The Wheatsheaf Pelaw Grange 0191 388 3104
The Barley Mow Browns Buildings 0191 410 4504

CYCLE SHOPS

Cestria Cycles 11 Ashfield Terrace - 0191 388 7535

C2C Features: the Penshaw Monument, a look-alike Doric Temple dedicated to Theseus, was built in memory of John George Lambton, the 1st Earl of Durham.

Be thankful to leave the river here for fear of the Lambton Worm! The legend runs that a young Lambton lad, fishing in the river against all advice, caught a small worm. In disgust he threw it into a nearby well and went off to fight in the Crusades. On his return the "worm" had grown into a dragon which ravaged the countryside. A witch agreed to slay the beast on condition that Lambton kill the first living thing he met. Unfortunately it was his father, whom of course he spared, and so failed to fulfil his side of the bargain, thus nine generations of Lambtons were condemned to meet untimely ends!

Chester-le-Street

Heather Rippon — Malling Guest House, 1 Oakdale Terrace, Chester-le-Street, DH2 2SU

Telephone **0191 3702571 Fax 0191 3701391**
E-mail: heather@mallingguesthouse.freeserve.co.uk
Rooms — 1 double + 1 single + 1 family
B&B — £17.00-£28.00
Packed lunch — £3.50
Distance from C2C — On route   Hotel has Public Bar
3 Diamonds. *"Experienced cyclist caterers. In small hamlet. Warm, friendly atmosphere. TV lounge, very comfortable."*

Lambton Worm Hotel — 52 North Road, Chester-le-Street, Co. Durham DH3 4AT*

Telephone — **0191 388 3386**
Rooms — 9 double + 4 single
B&B — £16.00-£28.00
Evening meals — £2.50-£15.00
Packed lunch — £3.50
Distance from C2C — On route   Hotel has Public Bar
ETB 2 Diamonds. *"13-bedroomed hotel/pub boasting 2 bars, excellent food, pool, darts, big-screen football. Tolerant understanding staff of muddy and exhausted bikers!"*

Beamish
Open Air Museum

SUNDERLAND

*Sunderland, once home of shipbuilding, coal-mining and glass making, became a city in 1992 and is just a stone's throw from the coast and the North Sea. **St Peter's Church**, built in 674 when Sunderland became established as one of England's earliest centres of Christianity, was notable as the first "glazed" building in England. George Washington's ancestral home is in **Washington village**, which is now part of the city of Sunderland: what an amazing connection with Whitehaven, the start of the C2C, where Washington's grandparents had their home!*

PLACES OF INTEREST

Washington Old Hall   In Washington village. George Washington's ancestral home 0191 416 6879

National Glass Centre   Demonstration of glass blowing & Throwing Stones Restaurant

Crowtree Leisure Centre   Town centre: have a celebratory swim - the sea could be a bit chilly! 0191 553 2600

EATING OUT

Marine Activity Centre   Trattoria Duo 0191 5100 600

Snow Goose Café   Good food & fun 0191 529 4091

CYCLE SHOPS

Peter Darke Cycles   113 High St West 0191 510 8155

For tourist and accommodation information on Newcastle, Tynemouth and Whitley Bay please turn to pages 92-95

Sunderland

Mrs Eileen Hughes
Brendon House, 49 Roker Park Road, Roker, Sunderland SR6 9PL

Telephone	**0191 548 9303**
e-mail	brendonhouse@hotmail.com
Rooms	1 double + 4 family + 1twin
B&B	£15.00-£20.00
Packed lunch	£3.25
Distance from C2C	½ mile Pub nearby

1 Diamonds *"5 minutes from Marine Centre and Seaburn Railway Station. Clean, comfortable, spacious rooms with TV, tea/coffee making-facilities. Ideal for weary travellers. Bike storage."*

Karen & Robin Dawson
Belmont Guest House, 8 St Georges Terrace, Roker, Sunderland SR6 9LX

Telephone	**0191 567 2438 or 0191 5140689**
Rooms	10 double + 2 single
B&B	£18.00-£30.00
Distance from C2C	On route Pub nearby

ETB 2 Diamonds. *"Small family-run guest-house. 100 yds from sea front and C2C route. En-suite rooms. Lock-up available for bikes. Warm welcome at the end of your ride."*

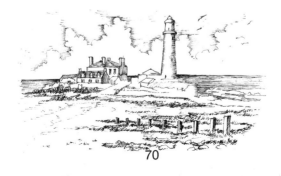

Camping & Caravan Sites

Workington

Pack Horse Camp Site: Low Seaton, Seaton, Workington, Cumbria, CA14 1PP. (at start & finish of C2C & Reivers Routes)Contact: John Bromley: **01900 603618**

Inglenook Caravan & Camping Park, Fitz Bridge, Lamplugh, Workington, CA14 4SH *(on C2C)* Tel/Fax **01946 861240**

Braithwaite

Scotgate Chalet, Camping & Caravan Holiday Park, Braithwaite, Keswick, Cumbria CA12 5TF *(C2C 100 yds)* Tel **017687 78343** *Fax 017687 78099*

Troutbeck

Gill Head Farm, Troutbeck, Penrith, Cumbria CA11 0ST Tel **017687 79652** *(See advertisement page 79.)*

Penruddock

Beckses Caravan & Camping Park, Penruddock, Penrith, Cumbria CA11 0RX *(c. ½ mile from C2C)* Tel **017684 83224**

Alston

Horse & Waggon Camping & Caravan Park, Nentsberry, Alston, Cumbria CA9 3LH, William Patterson *(swings on play area, WC and showers available, 3 miles south-east Alston on A689. Tents from £4.00, OS map ref NY 764 451)* Tel **01434 382805**

Rookhope

The Old Vicarage, Rookhope, Co Durham DL13 2AE Tel **01388 517375**

Hamsterley

Byreside Caravan Site, Hamsterley, Newcastle-upon-Tyne NE17 7RT, Mrs Val Clemitson *(between Ebchester and Hamsterley Mill, adjacent to Derwent Walk & Cycle Track)* Tel **01207 560280/560499**

Camping & Caravan Sites

Rowlands Gill

Derwent Park Caravan & Camping Site, Rowlands Gill, Tyne & Wear NE39 1LG. David Johnson *(discount for C2C cyclists. 100m from C2C Route)*

Tel/Fax **01207 543383 (see advertisement on page 85)**

Beamish

Bobby Shafto Caravan Park, Beamish, Co. Durham DH9 0RY *(adjacent to world famous Beamish Museum, only ¾ mile from C2C route)*

Tel **0191 370 1776** Fax 0191 456 1083

Bunk Houses

Penrith	Corney House. Mrs Mawer 01768 **867627**
Langwathby	The Hayloft. Mrs Peet **01768 881661**
Renwick	Half Way Bunkhouse, Busk Rigg Farm, Mrs Milburn **01768 898288**
Alston	St Paul's Mission, Townhead. **01434 382441**
Nenthead	Heritage Centre. **01434 382726**
	Miners Arms. **01434 381427**

Youth Hostels

YHA, Northern Region, PO Box 11, Matlock, Derbyshire DE4 2XA (inc SAE)

Tel **01629 825850** *(See advertisement page 83)*

Cockermouth Youth Hostel

Double Mills, Cockermouth, Cumbria CA13 0DS £4.95 (under 18s) £7.20 (adults) + Breakfast £2.95 Evening meal £4.40 *(on C2C route)*

Tel **01900 822561**

Skiddaw House Youth Hostel

Bassenthwaite, Keswick, Cumbria CA12 4QX £3.85 (under 18s) £5.65 (adults), self-catering only

Tel **016974 78325**

Keswick Youth Hostel

Station Road, Keswick, Cumbria CA12 5LH
£6.55 (under 18s) £9.75 (adults) + Breakfast £2.95 *Membership requirement: available at Hostel. (on C2C route)*
Tel **017687 72484**

Alston Youth Hostel

The Firs, Alston, Cumbria CA9 3RW   £5.40 (under 18s) £8.00 (adults) + Breakfast £2.95 *(2 miles from C2C route)*
Tel **01434 381509** Fax 01434 382401

Edmundbyers Youth Hostel

Low House, Edmundbyers, Consett, Co Durham DH8 9NL
£4.45 (under 18s) £6.50 (adults), self-catering only *(on C2C route)* Tel/Fax **01207 255651**

Consett YMCA

Parliament Street, Consett, Co. Durham DH8 5DH 12 rooms, 65 beds in Alpine style rooms. B&B £12.50. Evening meal £5.00. Packed lunch £3.00. OS Ref. 105 509. **(See advertisement page 83.)** Tel **01207 502680** Fax 01207 501578

Newcastle upon Tyne Youth Hostel

107 Jesmond Road, Newcastle upon Tyne NE2 1NJ
£5.15 (under 18s) £7.70 (adults) + Breakfast £2.85
Tel **0191 281 2570**

Camping Barns

Camping Barns are stone barns providing simple overnight shelter. They are roomy and dry, so there is no need to carry a tent. They have a wooden sleeping platform sometimes with mattresses. Tables, a slate cooking bench and cold water tap and WC are also provided together with a washing-up bowl, clothes hooks and waste bags.

Cumbria: for bookings at most of the Lake District National Park barns you must first ring Keswick Information Centre on **017687 72803**

Loweswater - Swallow Barn, Waterend Farm *(west end of Loweswater, on C2C route)* OS NY 116 226

Newlands Valley - Catbells Barn, *(c. 2 miles from C2C route)* OS NY 243 208

Keswick - Eagle's Nest Barn, Low Grove Farm, Millbeck, *(c. 2 miles from C2C route)* OS NY 258 259

Mungrisdale - Blake Beck Barn between Keswick and Penrith, *(c. 2 miles from C2C route)* OS NY 367 278

Renwick Half Way Bunk House. Phone **01768 898288**

Alston - Wearhead Camping Barn, Black Cleugh, Cowshill, Wearhead, Co. Durham DL13 1DJ *(c. 2 miles from C2C route)* Tel **01388 537 395** Mr Robert Walton OS NY 436 821

Useful Telephone Numbers

Weather News

Cumbria & the Lake District Weathercall	0891 500 419
North East England Weathercall	0891 500 418

Tourist Information Centres

Whitehaven	01946 852939
Keswick	017687 72645
Cockermouth	01900 822634
Penrith	01768 867466
Alston (April to October)	01434 381696
Stanhope	01388 527650
Beamish	0191 370 2533
Gateshead	0191 477 3478
Sunderland	0191 553 2000
Newcastle upon Tyne	0191 261 0610
Whitley Bay	0191 200 8535

Travel Information: Bus, Coach and Train

Stagecoach Cumberland	01946 63222
Cumbria County Council Travellink	01228 606000
Durham County Council Travellink	0191 383 3337
Tyne & Wear County Council Travellink	0191 232 5325
National Express	0990 808080
National Express Newcastle	0191 232 3300
National Rail Enquiries Line	0345 484 950
Scotrail Enquiries Line	0345 550 033
Cycle Booking Line NW Trains	0845 6040231

Bike Shops and Repairs

Whitehaven	Kershaw's Cycles, 125 Queen St 01946 590700
	Mark Taylor Cycles, 5/6 New St 01946 692252
Workington	Traffic Lights Bikes, 35 Washington St 01900 603283
	New Bike Shop, 18-20 Market Pl 01900 603337
Cockermouth	Wordsworth Hotel Bike Hire 01900 822757
	Derwent Cycles, 4 Market Place 01900 822113
Braithwaite	The Stores 017687 78273
Keswick	Keswick Mountain Bikes, Southey Hill 017687 75202
	Glaramara Guest House 017687 73216 (P.25)
Penrith	Arragons, 2 Brunswick Rd 01768 890344
	Harpers, 1-2 Middlegate 01768 864475
Alston	Nentholme B&B, The Butts 01434 381 523
Nenthead	Mark Fearn, blacksmith 01434 382194
Allenheads	Village Shop: essential bike spares
Stanhope	Weardale Mountain Bikes, Frosterley 01388 528129
Consett	Consett Cycle Co, 62 Medomsley Rd 01207 581 205
	McVickers Sports, Front St 01207 505 121
Stanley	Main Brothers, Front St 01207 290 258
Chester-le-St	Cestria Cycles, 11 Ashfield Terr 0191 3887535
Washington	Bike Shed, 3 Westview, Concord 0191 416 906
	Bike Rack, 65-66 In Shops 0191 419 1521
Metro Centre	The Bike Place, 8 Allison Court 0191 488 3137
Newcastle	Newcastle Cycle Centre, 165 Westgate Rd 0191 230 3022
Byker	Hardisty Cycles, 5 Union Rd 0191 265 8619
Sunderland	Darke Cycles, 113 High St W 0191 510 8155
	Cycle World, 118 High St West 0191 565 8188
Tynemouth	Cyclepath, 4 Queensway, 0191 258 6600

C2C Check List

Tool Kit

Chain splitter
Pump
Allen keys
Adjustable spanner
Screwdriver
Tyre levers
Spoke key
Strong tape (for quick repairs)
Chain & gear lubricant

Bike Spares

Puncture repair kit
Front and rear lights
Batteries
Spare chain links
Brake blocks
Straddle wire
Bike lock
Inner tube

Personal Kit

Wash kit
Money / credit card
Head torch
First aid kit
Liners for bags
Emergency rations
Water bottle
Survival bag
One change of clothes
Map & B&B Guide

Clothing

Towel
Cycle shorts (padded)
Cycle shirt/fleece top
Thermal vest
Helmet
Gloves
Fleece
Windproof top
Waterproof jacket
Waterproof trousers
Boots/shoes/trainers
Track suit bottoms
Underwear
3 pairs socks

Morven House Hotel

Siddick Road
Workington
Cumbria
CA14 1LE
Tel/Fax 01900 602118

Relaxed and informal atmosphere for guests. En-suite rooms. Good food. Ideal stop over for C2C participants. Start your tour in comfortable, detached house with car park and secure cycle storage. You may leave your car until your return if you wish.

"Take nothing but photographs
Leave nothing but tyre-tracks"

Glenlea House, Whitehaven

Don't miss the opportunity to sit on our terrace with an evening drink and enjoy magnificent views stretching as far as the eye can see from the harbour to the Isle of Man. We will take care of your car while you are away.

Mrs Oliver, Glenlea House, Lowca, Whitehaven, Cumbria CA28 6PS Tel 01946 693873 Fax 01946 694350

Gill Head Farm

Mrs J. Wilson
Gill Head Farm
Troutbeck
Penrith
Cumbria CA11 0ST
Tel 017687 79652

Bed and Breakfast + Camping. Stay in the comfortable 17th-century farmhouse with oak beams and log fires. Enjoy traditional home-cooking. All rooms are en-suite, with tea/coffee-making facilities, colour TV, and central heating throughout. For campers we have a level, sheltered campsite, with laundry and shop. The Troutbeck Inn is a 5 minute walk - bike no further!

ARRAGONS CYCLE CENTRE
2 Brunswick Road
Penrith

Your Coast to Coast Cycle Shop
For spares, repairs, wheel-building
and wheel repairs

Main agents for
**MARIN SARACEN DAWES
RALEIGH**

Any problems at all,
just give us a call

01768   890344

BEE COTTAGE FARM

**CASTLESIDE CONSETT
CO. DURHAM DH8 9HW
Tel Liz Lawson 01207 508224
Farmhouse Teas
Bed & Breakfast
Self-catering**

**A working farm with lovely views situated close to
the Waskerley Way**
(between points 105 and 106 on the C2C map.)

**Evening Meals and Packed Lunches available
Tea-Room open 1 - 6pm**

Good food - plenty of it!

**A warm, friendly welcome and home comforts
for individual cyclists, family groups
or even larger parties
Sleeps 34**

The "Wish You Were Here" TV team stayed with us whilst in the area when making the C2C film - *We hope you will too!*

"3 Diamonds"
*English
Tourist Board*

DERWENT PARK

CARAVAN AND CAMPING SITE
Rowlands Gill, Tyne and Wear NE39 1LG

An excellent site and location for the last night on the C2C,
by the River Derwent, and adjacent to the route. Excellent
showers and laundry facilities. Cycle lock-ups available. Pub
with food, village shops and services within 400 m.
Site managed by cycling enthusiasts.
For colour brochure write, telephone or fax:
The Warden (01207) 543383

THE ALLENHEADS TRUST
Allenheads Heritage Centre
Allenheads
Northumberland NE47 9UQ

Allenheads is England's highest village and is the ideal stopping
off place on the C2C route. The Trust is a registered Charity
which provides many facilities for tourists to enjoy. Visit the
Heritage Centre, Engine House, Blacksmith's Shop, Nature
Trail, or enjoy excellent food in the Hemel Café which caters for
cyclists. Also in the village are toilets, a pub and post office.
For a full colour brochure and list of accommodation please send
a SAE to the above address or

Telephone/Fax   01434 685043

The
Reivers
Cycle Route

A cycle Route
from
Tynemouth to Whitehaven

To be used with the official route map
available from Sustrans 0117 929 0888

Gina Farncombe

Curlew Press

The Reivers Cycle Route

This 150 mile cycle way runs from east to west coast with the gradients in the cyclist's favour. It winds its way through some of the wildest and most untouched countryside in the UK from the mouth of the mighty River Tyne to the Cumbrian coast. Along the way riders will follow the shores of beautiful Kielder Water before crossing the border for a brief foray into Scotland.

The Route has been named after the marauding family clans who terrorised northern England and the Scottish Borders in the 15th c. and 16th c. They lived by cattle rustling, kidnapping, arson and murder. The route passes many fortified farmhouses revealing the rich heritage of the area.

The Reivers Cycle Route gives the potential of a wonderful round trip by linking with the C2C at Whitehaven.

Start your holiday from home by leaving your car behind! There are frequent main line inter-city trains to and from Newcastle.

If at all possible, please book accommodation, meals and packed lunches in advance, and do not arrive unannounced expecting beds and meals to be available! If you have to cancel a booking, please give the proprietor as much notice as you can so that the accommodation can be re-let.

Note   Back-up vehicles are strongly advised to use main roads in order to keep the Reivers Cycle Route as traffic free as possible.

Contents

Accommodation
place names (east-west)

REIVERS CYCLE ROUTE - WESTERN HALF

.... England - Scotland border

N

0   10   20
      km

SOUTHERN UPLANDS

SCOTLAND

Hermitage
Castle ■

M74/A74

Newcastleton
Kershopefoot

Bailey Mill
Catlowdy

Bewcastle
Longtown   Kirkcambeck
              Hethersgill

Kirklinton

Walton ●

ENGLAND

CARLISLE

SOLWAY

FIRTH

Silloth ■

Dalston

M6

River Eden

Whelpo
Parkend   Caldbeck
Ireby ●   Newlands
             Hesket
MARYPORT   Newmarket
        Uldale   Fell Side

PENRITH

Seaton
COCKERMOUTH
WORKINGTON

Bassenthwaite Lake

KESWICK

M6

WHITEHAVEN

THE LAKE DISTRICT

——— main route
- - - alternative route
········· Cumbria Cycleway
▶▶▶▶ C-2-C route

90

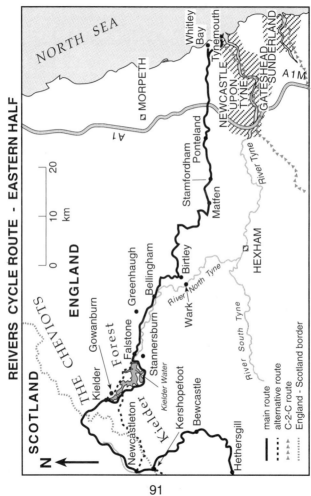

REIVERS CYCLE ROUTE - EASTERN HALF

N

SCOTLAND

THE CHEVIOTS

ENGLAND

NORTH SEA

Whitley Bay
Tynemouth
NEWCASTLE UPON TYNE
GATESHEAD
SUNDERLAND
A1M

MORPETH

A1

Ponteland
Stamfordham
Matfen

Birtley
Wark
River North Tyne

HEXHAM

River Tyne

River South Tyne

Kielder Forest
Kielder
Gowanburn
Greenhaugh
Bellingham
Falstone
Stannersburn
Kielder Water

Newcastleton
Kershopefoot
Bewcastle

Hethersgill

km
0   10   20

main route
alternative route
C-2-C route
England - Scotland border

NEWCASTLE

Newcastle can trace its beginnings to the river-crossing and fort which we know as the start of Hadrian's Wall. Later Robert, the son of William I, built a fort in 1080 and called it Newcastle. The shipping of coal and wool played a big part in the town's growth as a merchant and trading centre, and later ship-building and engineering were to employ a large part of the community.

TYNEMOUTH *owes its existence to the outcrop of hard sandstone which juts out between the Tyne and the sea defying the effects of wave and weather. Monks*

Earl Grey Monument

from the Holy Island of Lindisfarne came here in 627 and built the Priory which was one of the richest in the country and at one stage in its history monks were sent here as a reprimand for being disobedient. One poor exile wrote: "Shipwrecks are frequent and the poor people eat only a malodorous seaweed called 'slank' which they gather on the rocks, but the church is of wondrous beauty." *During the Roman occupation Tynemouth was an important supply port for Hadrian's Wall. In Victorian times people flocked here on the new railway to enjoy the sheltered bathing and boating.*

Tynemouth Priory

NEWCASTLE

PLACES OF INTEREST
Bagpipe Museum   Unusual and interesting
Laing Art Gallery   Holds very good exhibitions

PLACES TO EAT
"Crown Posada" Pub   On quayside: lively atmosphere
Café Procope   On quayside: good food and
                            popular with students

BIKE SHOPS and REPAIRS
Hardisty Bikes   5 Union Road 0191 510 8155
Dentons   Blenheim St 0191 232 3903

TYNEMOUTH

PLACES OF INTEREST
The Castle and Priory   Great atmosphere
Sea Life Centre   Excellent displays

PLACES TO EAT
Land of Green Ginger   Home-made food café
Porters Café   Tynemouth Station

OUTDOOR EQUIPMENT
Outdoor World   Whitley Bay, good stock
                            of outdoor equipment

Tynemouth and Whitley Bay

Stuart	Avalon Hotel, 26 South Parade,
Collingwood	Whitley Bay, Tyne & Wear NE26 2RG
Telephone	**0191 251 0080** Fax 0191 251 0100
e-mail	reception@avalon-hotel.freeserve.co.uk
Rooms	3 single + 2 double + 1 twin + 8 family
B&B	£25.00-£40.00
Evening Meal	Available Packed lunch £3.00
Distance from route	On route Pub 20 yds

2 Diamonds ETB *"Come this way - start/finish in Whitley Bay. Cyclist-friendly family-run hotel. All rooms en-suite. Bar, restaurant. **Free pint to every one who finishes the C2C!**"*

Mrs M. Ruddy	York House Hotel, 28/32 Park Parade,
	Whitley Bay, Tyne & Wear NE26 1DX
Telephone	**0191 252 8313 Fax 0191 251 3953**
e-mail	reservations@yorkhousehotel.com
Rooms	1 single + 12 double + 5 twin + 7 family
B&B	£20.00-£35.00
Evening meal	£12.50 Packed lunch £5.00
Distance Route	On route Pubs nearby

4 Diamonds RAC & AA *"Delightful family run en-suite accommodation with the benefit of new studios for 2001. Secure bike storage and onsite laundry facilities."*

Tynemouth and Whitley Bay

Hilary Thompson   Marlborough Hotel,20 - 21 East
                       Parade, Whitley Bay NE26 1AP
Telephone   **0191 251 3628**   Fax 0191 252 5033
e-mail   reception@marlborough-hotel.com
Rooms   15 double/single/twin *(most en-suite)*
B&B   £22.00-£30.00
Evening meal   £11.95   Packed lunch £5.00
Distance from Route   On route Pubs nearby

4 Diamonds ETC & AA *"Family run hotel in prime position on Whitley Bay seafront. Excellent accommodation with bike parking available."*

Doreen Jack   Lindsay Guest House, 50 Victoria
                       Avenue, Whitley Bay NE26 2BA
Telephone   **0191 252 7341**   Fax 0191251 6899
E-mail   info@lindsayguesthouse.co.uk
Web site   www.lindsayguesthouse.co.uk
Rooms   2 double + 2 twin + 2 family
B&B   £25.00-£35.00 *(all rooms en-suite)*
Packed lunch   £4.00
Distance from Route   On route Pubs & restaurants nearby

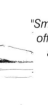

"Small family run guest house offering quality en-suite rooms and safe cycle store."

Stamfordham

Mrs V. Fitzpatrick   Church House, Stamfordham,
Northumberland NE18 0PB

Telephone	**01661 886736** **Mobile 07889 312623**
e-mail bedandbreakfast@stamfordham.fsbusiness.co.uk	
Rooms	2 doubles + single
B&B	£22.00
Packed lunch	£3.50-£4.00 Distance from route
On route	Pub nearby

"Pretty village green, old village pubs. 17th-c cream painted stone house of great character on south side of green, private residence. Good breakfast, welcoming hosts."

Wark

This little village is very near the Reivers Route. It has a shop, post office and a pub. The landlord will direct you via a scenic and traffic free lane back onto the Route again.

Bob Rowland   Battlesteads Hotel, Wark, Hexham,
Northumberland NE48 3LS

Telephone	**01434 230209 Fax 01434 230730**
E-mail	**info@battlesteads-hotel.co.uk**
Rooms	4 doubles + 3 twin + 2 family + 1 single
B&B	£30.00-£35.00 Ev. meal from £18.45
Packed lunch	£3.50
Distance from route	1 mile (turn left at Birtley)

3 Diamonds

"A converted 17th-c farmhouse carefully modernised to provide comfortable and friendly surroundings. Very used to having cyclists and will help with repairs. "

BELLINGHAM

This ancient little market town, known locally as "Bellin-jum", nestles at the foot of some of the wildest and most barren fells in Northumberland. There are medieval references to Bellingham Castle belonging to the King of Scotland's forester, but sadly no trace remains.

Bellingham Bridge

St Cuthbert's Church is unique with its stone roof and extremely narrow windows. Both features were some defence against the marauding Scots who twice burnt it to the ground. In its graveyard lies the famous "Long Pack" which is responsible for one of Northumbrian's most notorious tales of murder, intrigue and deception.

PLACES OF INTEREST
Hareshaw Linn — Superb waterfall, ½ mile walk
St Cuthbert's Well — Reputed to be healing water - especially for sore cyclists!

PLACES TO EAT
The Cheviot Hotel — Restaurant and bar meals
Fountain Tea Room — Good cheese scones!

BIKE REPAIRS
Village Country Store — Do hold some spare parts
01434 220027

Bellingham

Mr and Mrs T.V. Forster Crofters End, The Croft, Bellingham, Hexham, Northumberland NE48 2JY

Telephone | **01434 220034**
Rooms | 1 single + 1 double + 1 twin/family
B&B | £16.00-£18.00
Packed lunch | £3.50 *(prior notice please)*
Distance from route | 100 yds   Pub ½ mile

(No smoking please.) "End terrace family home on outskirts of village. Homely ex-farming family. Pennine Way passes the gate. We like our walkers and cyclists best! "

Joyce Gaskin 'Lyndale' Guest House, Bellingham, Northumberland NE48 2AW

Telephone/Fax | **01434 220361**
e-mail | **ken&joy@lyndalegh.fsnet.co.uk**
Rooms | 1 single + 2 double + 1 twin + family
B&B | £23.50-£25.00 *(no smoking please)*
Evening meal | £12.50   Packed lunch £3.50
Distance from route | On route   Pub nearby

4 Diamonds *"Quality en-suites. Big breakfast menu. Panoramic views. Bike wash & storage. Laundry facilities. Veggies welcome. Walled garden, patio, gazebo and fountain. Private car park."*

Simon & Julie Kennedy 'The Cheviot Hotel, Main Street, Bellingham, Northumberland NE48 2AU

Telephone/Fax | **01434 220696**
Rooms | 1 single + 2 double + 3 twin
B&B | £22.50-£25.00
Evening meal | from £3.50-£12.50.Packed lunch £3.50
Distance from route | On route   Pub nearby

3 Diamonds *"Situated on the C2C route. Secure overnight cycle storage. All bedrooms en-suite with tea/coffee making facilities. Lounge bar and restaurant. Sunday Carvery."*

FALSTONE

This secluded little hamlet lost nearly 80% of its parish under the waters of Kielder Reservoir. Today the village is a tranquil beauty spot surrounded by trees, and a good stopping place for the cyclist with post office, shop and pub. A tributary to the Tyne bubbles its way through the centre of the village and, depending on the time of year, it is possible to see dippers, heron, cormorants, goosanders, and with luck you may witness the miraculous sight of salmon spawning.

The Village Hall   Teas. Floor-sleeping space, cooking and washing facilities
                          Andy McMillan 01434 240224

Post Office   Mrs Entwisle

The Blackcock   Old world pub with good food

Falstone

Robin Kershaw   The Pheasant Inn, Stannersburn,
                      Falstone, Kielder Water,
                      Northumberland NE48 1DD
Telephone/Fax   **01434 240382**
e-mail   **thepheasantinn@kielderwater.demon.co.uk**
Rooms   4 doubles + 3 twins + 1 family
B&B   from £30.00
Evening meal   £10.00-£18.00 3-course meal
Packed lunch   £5.00 Distance from route   1 mile
(No smoking in bedrooms and dining room please.)
4 Diamonds. *"A traditional country Inn, bursting with charac-
ter. Stone walls, beams and open fires provide its cosy at-
mosphere. Real ale, good home-cooking, all rooms en-suite."*

Andy McMillan   Falstone Village Hall, Falstone, Hexham,
                      Northumberland NE48 1BB
Telephone   **01434 240224**
*Floor space available for groups of up to 25 people. Showers,
toilets, washing and cooking facilities. Bring your own sleeping
bag and roll mat. Minimum charge £25.00 for up to 20 people.*

Peter and Linda   The Blackcock Inn, Falstone, Hexham,
  Laws   Nr Kielder, Northumberland NE48 1AA
Telephone/Fax   **01434 240200**
e-mail   **blackcock@falstone.fsbusiness.co.uk**
Rooms   2 double + 2 twin + 1 family
B&B   £20.00-£25.00
Evening meal   £3.95-£9.95   Packed lunch £3.50
Distance from route   On route   Public bar
(No smoking in dining-room or bedrooms please) **3 Diamonds**
*"Olde world country pub with good home cooked food, real ale,
comfortable accommodation. Log fires. Walkers & cyclists
warmly welcomed. Bike storage available."*

Falstone

John and Shirley Richardson High Yarrow Farm, Falstone, Hexham
Northumberland NE48 1BG
Telephone **01434 240264**
Rooms 1 twin + 1 single *(no smoking please)*
B&B £16.00 Packed lunch £3.00
(prior notice for packed lunch please)
Distance from route ¼ mile Pubs nearby
Listed Commended. *"150-year-old farmhouse on working farm situated at the foot of Kielder Water in the hamlet of Yarrow. Happy to offer transport to the pub if needed"*

Mrs Karen Hodgson Ridge End Farm & Cottage, Falstone,
nr Kielder Water, Hexham, NE48 1DE
Telephone **01434 240395**
Rooms 1 twin + 1 family *(both en-suite)*
B&B £20.00 *(no smoking please)*
Evening meal No Packed lunch £3.00
Distance from route ½ mile Pub nearby
4 Diamonds *"This is a magnificent 16th-c bastel house (a fortified farmhouse). It is the historic home of border reivers and has 5ft thick walls. Private lounge available for guests with roaring log fires. There is a cottage available also."*

KIELDER WATER

A wild and romantic place, Kielder Water is the heart of Border Reiver country. It is hard to imagine the cattle rustling, kidnapping and arson that flourished here in the 15th and 16th centuries. Today Kielder's stunning scenery, peace and quiet welcome all visitors. There is a wealth of facilities for the cyclist here. Northumbria Water, who created the reservoir, has been responsible for a good deal of the inspiration behind the Reivers Cycle Route.

PLACES OF INTEREST
Tower Knowe Visitor Centre
An Information Centre with extensive gift shop and audio visual exhibition. Situated on south bank very near the dam wall.

Leaplish Waterside Park
Heated swimming pool and sauna, campsite, accommodation together with a licensed restaurant, sculpture trail, bird of prey centre, and much more.

KIELDER VILLAGE

Kielder Castle

Situated at the head of the reservoir Kielder was once in a wild and uncultivated country surrounded by moors and bogs. It is now a purpose-built forestry village cocooned by alpine spruce and pine trees. Before the turn of the century Kielder Castle, which stands guard over the village, would have been hidden and alone at the valley head. It was built in 1775 by the Duke of Northumberland as his hunting lodge. Shooting parties travelled from London on the sleeper and were met at the station by pony and trap. To carry home a bag of 200 brace of grouse and blackcock in a day was not unusual. The village is a small oasis for the cyclist with a shop, pub and post office.

PLACES OF INTEREST
Kielder Castle Forest Shop, tea room, WCs
  Park Information Centre 01434 250209

PLACES TO EAT
The Anglers Arms 01434 250234

BIKE SHOPS Ken and Kim Bone, opposite the
Kielder Bikes Castle **Tel. 01434 250392**

REIVERS CYCLE ROUTE - Kielder Water area

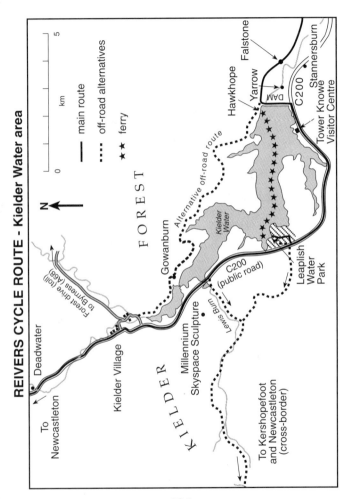

Legend:
— main route
···· off-road alternatives
★ ★ ferry

Deadwater

To Newcastleton

Forest drive (toll) to Byrness (A68)

KIELDER FOREST

Kielder Village

Gowanburn

Alternative off-road route

Millennium Skyspace Sculpture

Kielder Water

C200 (public road)

Lewis Burn

To Kershopefoot and Newcastleton (cross-border)

Leaplish Water Park

Hawkhope

Yarrow

DAM

Falstone

Stannersburn

C200

Tower Knowe Visitor Centre

Kielder

Rachel Cowper

Calvert Trust Kielder, Kielder Water, Hexham, Northumberland NE48 1BS

Telephone	**01434 250232** Fax 01434 250 015
E-mail	enquires@calvert.kielder.com
Rooms	20 twin + 4 family
B&B	£17.50
Evening meal	£7.50 Packed lunch £3.50
Distance from route	On route Pub 4 miles

Chalets - 5 Keys. *"The Calvert Trust at Kielder offers accessible accommodation for individuals, groups or families, situated close to both routes, half-way between Falstone and Kielder. Ideal situation for the cycle route."*

Julia Scott

Leaplish Waterside Park, Kielder Water, Northumberland NE48 1BT

Telephone	**01434 250312** Fax 01434 250 806
e-mail	kielder.water@nwl.co.uk
Rooms	2 Dormitories *(sleep 8 people in each)* + 2 double rooms + family room
Accommodation	£12.00-£20.00*(breakfasts additional)*
Evening meal	from £5.50 Packed lunch from £5.00
Distance from route	On route Pub nearby

*The Reivers rest Bunkbarn on the Reivers Route. Budget accommodation in stunning lakeside setting. Adjacent to excellent facilities and swimming pool."***(see advertisement on page 126)**

Kielder

Mrs Fiona Hall   Deadwater Farm, Kielder, Hexham, Northumberland NE48 1EW

Telephone	**01434 250216**
Rooms	1 double + 1 twin + 1 family
B&B	£17.00 *(no smoking - only in lounge)*
Evening meal	Snack £4.00 Packed lunch £3.00
Distance from route	100 yds Pub 2½ miles

4 Diamonds **ETB.** *"Old stone-built farmhouse in peaceful surroundings on Scotland/England border. It is recommended to eat on way here, unless you require a small meal. Bunk house at Leaplish too!"*

Mrs Janet Scott   Gowanburn, Kielder, Hexham, Northumberland NE48 1HL

Telephone	**01434 250254**
Rooms	1 double + 1 twin + 1 family
B&B	£16.50-£17.50
Evening meal	Light meal Packed lunch £2.50
Distance from route	On route Pub 1½ miles

2 Diamond ETB *"Superb views, peaceful old farmhouse on edge of Kielder Water. A beautiful place to stay deep in the forest of Kielder and a very friendly welcome."*

NEWCASTLETON

Newcastleton, with its broad Georgian streets and open squares, was purpose designed and built from scratch by the Duke of Buccleugh in 1792. Due to the changes in agriculture there was a need for more village-based employment such as handloom weaving. The houses were built with large windows to let in light for the new cottage industries.

The town has a **post office,** several pubs, an antique shop, a **bank**, a **grocery** and several guest-houses. Also the garage will help with **bike repairs** and there is also the interesting **LiddesdaleHeritage Centre.** If your time and energy allow don't miss a short detour to **Hermitage Castle.** This mys-

terious and magical place not only witnessed long years of turbulent border reiving, but it played host to the tragic Mary Queen of Scots when she snatched two hours' rendezvous with her lover Boswell.

Hermitage Castle

Newcastleton

Helen Rabour	Woodside, North Hermitage Street, Newcastleton,Roxburghshire TD9 0RZ
Telephone/Fax	**013873 75431**
E-mail:	hrabour@yahoo.co.uk
Room	2 double + 2 twin + 1 single
B&B	£17.00-£19.00
Evening meal	from £2.50 Packed lunch £3.50
Distance from route	On route Pub nearby

"Large house at north end of village. Spacious rooms with good beds & good food. Licensed. Also safe bike storage."

Bailey Mill

Mrs Pamela Copeland	Bailey Mill Accommodation & Trekking, Bailey, Newcastleton, Roxburghshire TD9 0TR
Telephone/Fax	**016977 48617**
e-mail	**lindastenhouse@virgin.co.uk**
Rooms	2 single + 4 double + 4 twin + 2 family
B&B	£20.00-£22.00
Evening meal	£8.00 Packed lunch £3.50
Distance from route	On route Pub on site

2 Star Commended. "*Courtyard apartments for self-catering or B&B. Relax in our jacuzzi, sauna, steam shower. Delicious home cooked meals and friendly atmosphere has attracted numerous cyclists to return with family or other groups.*"
(See advertisement on page 127)

Bailey Mill

BEWCASTLE

The famous Bewcastle Cross has survived 1300 years of relentless border weather in St Cuthbert's churchyard. The church and remains of the castle stand remote and almost alone save for a farmhouse in this forgotten outpost in a great sweep of wild and rugged countryside. There is a display of interpretative panels nearby in the small **Past & Present Heritage Centre.** They tell the story of the Anglo-Saxon cross. The runic inscriptions and carving are of a very high quality for this period in history.

'Summer is for grazing, but autumn is for raiding'

Just like football, our raiding friends were far too busy tending crops and fattening the cattle in summer to be doing any reiving, but as soon as the crops were gathered and the horses fit they would be hot foot across whichever border to get down to the serious winter business of stealing each other's wives, girl-friends, cattle, sheep and carefully-stored winter goods again.

Catlowdy near Longtown

Jack and Margaret Sisson	Bessietown Farm Country Guesthouse, Catlowdy, Longtown, Carlisle CA6 5QP
Telephone/Fax	**01228 577219 + 5772019**
E-mail	**bestbb2001@cs.com**
Rooms	2 single + 4 double + 4 twin + 2 family
B&B	£25.00-£33.00 *(no smoking please)*
Evening meal	£12.50 *(Small Bar on premise)*
Distance from route	1½ miles Pub 6 miles

5 Diamonds. *"Best B&B Cumbria and England Award winner. Warm welcome and delicious food. All rooms en-suite. Indoor heated swimming pool summer months. Open all year. Lockable storage. Drying facilities."*

Hethersgill

Georgina and John Elwen	New Pallyards, Hethersgill, Nr Carlisle, Cumbria CA6 6HZ
Telephone/Fax	**01228 577308**
E-mail	**info@newpallyards.freeserve.co.uk**
Rooms	2 double + 4 twin + 1 family *(en-suite)*
B&B	£22.00-£23.00
Evening meal	£13.00
Packed lunch	£4.00
Distance from route	1 mile Pub on site

4 Diamonds. *"Farmhouse accommodation & self catering cottages. visit our web site:* **www.newpallyards.freeserve.co.uk** *Residential licence, cycles undercover, large groups welcome. National Gold Award."*

Kirkcambeck

Marjorie Stobart

Cracrop Farm, Kirkcambeck,
nr Brampton, Cumbria CA8 2BW

Telephone **016977 48245**
Fax 016977 48333
E-mail **cragcrop@aol.com**
Rooms 1 single + 2 double + 1 twin *(all en-suite)*
B&B £25.00-£27.50 *(no smoking please)*
Packed lunch £4.00 *(prior notice please)*
Distance from route 1½ miles   Pub 3 miles *(lifts available)*
3 Diamonds Highly Commended. *"A warm welcome to our comfortable farmhouse. Luxuriously-appointed spacious bedrooms, TV and drinks tray, relax in the sauna (small extra charge) or spa bath. Superb traditional English breakfast. Transport available to pub."*

Askerton Castle

Walton

Mrs Una Armstrong

Town Head Farm, Walton,
nr Brampton, Cumbria CA8 2DJ

Telephone **016977 2730**
Rooms 1 double + 1 family
B&B £15.00-£16.00 *(no smoking please)*
Evening meal from £9.00
Packed lunch £3.00
Distance from route On route   Pub 200 yards
3 Diamonds *"Cosy farmhouse overlooks village green of Walton with spectacular views of Pennines and Lakeland Hills. Bar meals at Centurion Pub built on Hadrian's Wall."*

Kirklinton

Margaret Harrison	Clift House Farm, Kirklinton, (Near Smithfield) Carlisle, Cumbria, CA6 6DE.
Telephone	**01228 675237**
Mobile	07790758272
Rooms	1 double + 2 twin
B&B	£18.00-£20.00 Evening meal £10.00
Pub	Nearby
Distance from route	On route

ETB 3 Diamonds *"Spacious friendly farmhouse on the banks of the river Lyne. Beautiful walks and fishing. Complimentary tea and home baking on arrival. Brochure available."*

Westlinton

Jan Butler	Lynebank Guest House, Westlinton, nr Carlisle, Cumbria CA6 6AA
Telephone	**01228 792820 Fax 01228 792820**
E-mail	**infor@lynebank.co.uk**
Rooms	3 single + 7 double + 2 family + 1 twin
B&B	£18.00-£24.00
Evening meal	£10.00 Packed lunch £3.50
Distance from route	¼ miles Pub 2½ miles

4 Diamonds ETB *"Friendly family run licensed guest house, excellent home cooking, Bar, bar meals, vegetarian meals by request. All rooms en-suite."*

CARLISLE

This great border city greets its guests with open arms, but not so many years ago any visitor would have been treated with suspicion. It was the nerve-centre for bitter feuds and bloody battles created by the long-running dispute over the border betwen England and Scotland. Early in its history it was an important Roman headquarters for Hadrian's Wall. In 1092 William the Conqueror's son started to build the castle where later the unfortunate Mary Queen of Scots was incarcerated.

PLACES OF INTEREST

Tullie House Museum and Art Gallery	Excellent audio-visual interpretation of the Border Reivers
Carlisle Castle	Medieval dungeons, exhibitions
Carlisle Cathedral	Founded in 1122, fine wood carving and wall panels

PLACES TO EAT

The GrapeVine	Excellent, value for money, vegetarian food 01228 546617
Ottakars	**Town centre. Exciting & novel book shop with excellent cafe.**

BIKE REPAIRS

Palace Cycle	122 Botchergate 01228 523142
Scotby Cycles	Bridge St 01228 546931

Carlisle

Geoff and Elaine Webster	Angus Hotel, 14 Scotland Road, Carlisle CA3 9DG
Telephone	**01228 523546 Fax 01228 531895**
e-mail	**angus@hadrians-wall.fsnet.co.uk**
Rooms	3 single + 4 double + 3 family + 4 twin
B&B	£20.00-£42.00
Evening meal	£5.00-£15.00 Pck. lunch £3.50-£5.00
Distance from route	On route

(Mainly a non-smoking hotel.) **4 Diamonds.** *"Cosy Victorian town house offering personal hospitality, superb food in Almonds Bistro, local cheeses, home-baked bread and draught beer. Secure car parking and cycle storage."*
(See advertisement on page 126)

Eric and Daphne Houghton	Cherry Grove, 87 Petteril Street, Carlisle, Cumbria CA1 2AW
Telephone/Fax	**01228 541942**
e-mail	**petteril87@aol.com**
Rooms	2 double + 3 twin
B&B	£19.00-£20.00
Packed lunch	£4.25
Distance from route	On route Pub nearby

3 Diamonds *"Comfortable family run guest house with newly refurbished rooms .All rooms en-suite with all facilities including hairdryer and satellite TV. Good English breakfast, easy walking distance from city centre."*

Carlisle

Sheila Nixon   No. 1 Etterby Street Carlisle,
Cumbria CA3 9JB

Telephone/Fax   **01228 547285**
Rooms   1 double + 2 single rooms
B&B   £18.00-£20.00 *(no smoking please)*
Evening meal   £8.00-£10.00 *(prior notice please)*
Packed lunch   £4.00
Distance from route   On route   Pub nearby

3 Diamonds *"We are a Victorian guest house within easy distance of the city centre. There is secure cycle storage and we offer good wholesome food and a warm welcome will await you."*

Tina Murray   Parkland Guest House, 136 Petteril
Street,Carlisle, Cumbria CA1 2AW.

Telephone/Fax   **01228 548331**
Rooms   2 double + 3 twin + 1 family room
B&B   £17.50-£20.00
Packed lunch   £6.00
Distance from route   On route   Pub nearby

3 Diamonds *"Comfortable family run guest house with newly refurbished rooms .All rooms en-suite with all facilities including hairdryer and Satellite TV. Good English breakfast. We are within easy walking distance of the city centre. Very near bus and train stations."*

Prior Slee's Gateway
Carlisle Cathedral

Orton - Carlisle

Susan Harper

	Hazeldean Guest House, Orton Grange, Wigton Road, Carlisle,Cumbria CA3 9JB
Telephone/Fax	**01228 711953**
Rooms	2 double + 2 single rooms
B&B	£19.00
Evening meal	from £7.00 *(prior notice please)*
Packed lunch	£3.00
Distance from route	On route Pub nearby

3 Diamonds *"Friendly family run guest house set in extensive gardens.*
Offering home cooking, table licence and comfortable lounge.
Alternative therapies available on site, Massage Reflexology and Reiki - give yourself a treat!"

Sowerby Row

Liz & David Townsend

	Bluebell House, Sowerby Row, nr Carlisle, Cumbria CA4 0QQ
Telephone	**016974 76641**
E-mail	**david.townsend@talk21.com**
Rooms	2 double *(en-suite)*
B&B	£18.00-£22.00
Evening meal	£9.00 *(prior notice)*
Packed lunch	£3.50*(prior notice)*
Distance from route	On route

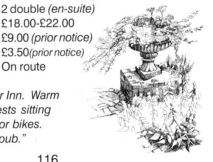

"A 250 year old former Inn. Warm and friendly with guests sitting room. Safe storage for bikes. Transport to the local pub."

THE EASTERN FELLS OF THE LAKE DISTRICT
NATIONAL PARK

Tread softly as you pass through this miraculously untouched corner of England!

St Mungo hurried here in the 6th century, for he had heard muffled whispers that word of the Gospels had not reached the ears of the wild and unruly people living in the Eastern Fells! Many of the local churches are named after his other more formal name, St Kentigern.

HESKET NEWMARKET

Ask a local inhabitant the name of an ash tree and he will tell you it is a 'Hesh'. Hesket means the place of the ash trees. Local farmers bought and sold bulls at the market cross. A generous village green invites travellers to taste the local brewed beer and rest awhile. There is a well stocked village shop, a post office, pub and several guest-houses. The Crown Inn is famous for its own home-brewed ales. They are named after local fells: Blencathra, Great Cock-up, and Doris in honour of the landlord's mother on her 90th birthday.

Hesket-New-Market

Mrs Monkhouse   Denton House, Hesket-New-Market,
or Mrs Armstrong   nr Caldbeck, Cumbria CA7 8JG
Telephone   **016974 78415**
E-mail   **dentonhnm@aol.com**
Rooms   1 single + 2 double + 1 twin + 3 family
B&B   £18.00-£25.00
Evening meal   From £9.00
Packed lunch   £2.50 *(prior notice please)*
Distance from route On route
Pub   Nearby *(with own brewery)*

"We have comfortable en-suite rooms with tea & coffee making facilities. Situated next door to The Old Crown who brew their own real ales"

Mrs Dorothy   Newlands Grange, Hesket-New-
  Studholme   Market, nr Wigton, Cumbria CA7 8HP
Telephone   **016974 78676**
Rooms   1 single + 2 double + 2 twin/family
B&B   £16.50-£19.50
Evening meal   From £7.50   Packed lunch £3.00
Distance from route On route   Pub 1½ miles

"Newlands Grange is a working farm looking onto the Caldbeck Fells, house featuring old oak beams and open fire. Good home-cooking and a warm welcome awaits all."

CALDBECK

Named after the river (Cold-beck), Caldbeck was a thriving rural industrial centre before steam-power and the Industrial Revolution. There is still a clog-maker in the village centre. In 1800 there were no fewer than 8 water-powered mills making bobbins, woollens and grinding corn.

__The Priests Mill__ which has been beautifully restored houses a craft centre, display area and restaurant with a picture gallery. In the churchyard is John Peel's grave , the famous Cumbrian Huntsman, and that of Mary, the Beauty of Buttermere who was the subject of the novel 'The Maid of Buttermere' by Melvyn Bragg.

PLACES OF INTEREST

The Howk A hidden gem upstream from the village
The Clog Maker Will Strong: next to the bridge

PLACES TO EAT

Priests Mill Delicious vegetarian food: you'll return!
Odd Fellows Arms Wholesome country food

After Caldbeck the route winds its way round the fell: an area known locally as Back 'a Skiddaw. __Parkend Restaurant__ and __The Snooty Fox__ are the only watering holes for several miles.

Caldbeck

Mrs Nan Savage   Swaledale Watch, Whelpo, nr Caldbeck,
                     Wigton, Cumbria CA7 8HQ.

Telephone/Fax   **016974 78409**
Rooms   2 double + 1 twin + 2 family
B&B   £17.00-£21.00
Evening meal   £11.00 *(prior notice please)*
Packed lunch   £3.50 approx *(prior notice please)*
Distance from route On route   Pub 1 mile

AA Selected QQQQ. *"Enjoy great comfort in beautiful surroundings on our working farm. A warm welcome, hot bath and good food await you. First there gets the Jacuzzi!"*

Mrs C. Slinger   Parkend Restaurant & Country Hotel,
                     nr Caldbeck, Wigton, Cumbria CA7 8HH.

Telephone   **016974 78494**   Fax 016974 78580
Rooms   4 double + 2 twin
B&B   £25.00-£32.00
Evening meal   £4.50-£20.00 Packed lunch £4.50
Distance from route ¼ mile   Licensed bar

(No smoking in dining room please.) **2 Star Hotel** *"17th-c farmhouse restaurant with quality en-suite rooms. Fine food in tranquil surroundings. Lock up bike park."*

**For tourist information and accommodation in
Cockermouth please turn to pages 18 - 20**

Youth Hostels

YHA, Northern Region, PO Box 11, Matlock, Derbyshire
DE4 2XA (inc SAE) *(See advertisement page 128.)*
Tel **01629 825850**

Newcastle-upon-Tyne Youth Hostel
107 Jesmond Road, Newcastle-upon-Tyne, NE2 1NJ
£5.15 (under 18s), £7.70 (adults) + Breakfast £2.85
Tel **0191 281 2570**

Once Brewed Youth Hostel
Military Road, Bardon Mill, Hexham, Northumberland
NE47 7AN £5.70 (under 18s), £8.50 (adults)
Tel **01434 344360**

Bellingham Youth Hostel
Woodburn Road, Bellingham, Hexham, Northumberland
NE48 2ED £4.25 (under 18s), £6.25 (adults)
Tel **01434 220313**

Carlisle Campus (University of Northumbria)
Old Brewery Residences, Bridge Lane, Caldewgate, Carlisle
CA2 5SW (available July 15-September 13)
Tel **01228 597352**

Carrock Fell Youth Hostel
High Row Cottage, Haltcliffe, Hesket Newmarket, Wigton,
Cumbria CA7 8JT £4.75 (under 18s), £6.95 (adults)
Tel **016974 78325**

Cockermouth Youth Hostel
Double Mills, Cockermouth, Cumbria CA13 0DS
£4.75 (under 18s), £6.95 (adults)
Tel **01900 822561**

Camping and Caravan Sites

BELLINGHAM
Brown Rigg   01434 220175
The Main Farm   01434 220258
FALSTONE
The Village Hall   01434 40343

KIELDER
Leaplish   01434 250278
Kielder Village   01434 250291

NEWCASTLETON
The Lidalia Caravan/Camp   01387 375203

LONGTOWN
Oakbank Lakes Country Park   01228 791108
High Gaitle   01228 791819

CARLISLE
West View, Grinsdale Bridge   01228 526336
Orton Grange (with swimmingpool)   01228 710252

DALSTON
Dalston Hall   01228 710165
HESKET NEW MARKET
Greenhill, Mrs Joan Todhunter   016974 78453
CALDBECK
Friars Hall   016974 78633

BEWALDETH
North Lakes   017687 76510
COCKERMOUTH
Violet Bank   01900 822169

Useful Telephone Numbers

Weather News

North East England Weathercall	0891 500 418
Cumbria & the Lake District Weathercall	0891 500 419

Tourist Information Centres

Gateshead	0191 477 3478
Newcastle-upon-Tyne	0191 261 0610
Whitley Bay	0191 200 8535
Hawick	01450 372547
Bellingham	01434 220616
Kielder	01434 240398
Longtown	01228 792835
Carlisle	01228 625600
Cockermouth	01900 822634
Silloth-on-Solway	01697 331944
Whitehaven	01946 695678
Maryport	01900 813738

Travel Information: Bus, Coach and Train

Northumberland County Council	01670 533128
Tyne & Wear County Council Travellink	0191 232 5325
Stagecoach Cumberland	01946 63222
National Express	0990 808080
National Express Newcastle	0191 232 3300
National Rail Enquiries Line	0345 484 950
Scotrail Enquiries Line	0345 550033
Cycle Booking Line NW Trains	0161 228 5906

How to get Home

Holiday Lakeland *(see inside cover)*	016973 71871
Stanley Taxis *(see page 86)*	01207 237424
Ted Gilman *(see page 125)*	0191 284 7534

Bike Shops and Repairs

Tynemouth Cyclepath, 14 Queensway 0191 258 6600

Metro Centre The Bike Place, 8 Allison Court 0191 488 3137

Newcastle Newcastle Cycle Centre, 165 Westgate Rd
0191 230 3022
Dentons, Blenheim St 0191 232 3903

Byker Hardisty Cycles, 5 Union Rd 0191 265 8619

Bellingham Village and Country Store do some
spare

parts 01434 220027

Kielder Kielder Castle, Ken and Kim Bone
01434 250392

Carlisle Mike Lee, Palace Cycle Stores, 122 Botchergate
01228 523142
Scotby Cycles, Bridge Street
01228 546931

Cockermouth Derwent Cycles 01900 822113
The Wordsworth Hotel
Bike Hire 01900 822757

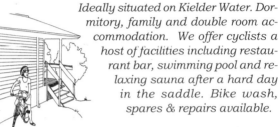

"Take nothing but photographs
Leave nothing but tyre-tracks"